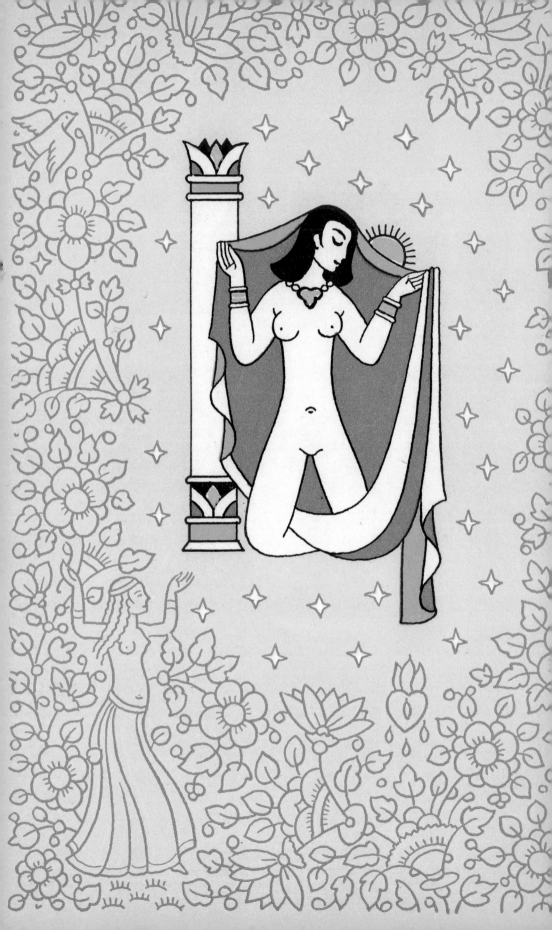

salome

A TRAGEDY IN ONE ACT
TRANSLATED FROM THE FRENCH OF
OSCAR WILDE
BY LORD ALFRED DOUGLAS
WITH A NEW INTRODUCTION
BY HOLBROOK JACKSON
DECORATED & HAND-ILLUMINATED
BY VALENTI ANGELO
FOR THE HERITAGE PRESS
NEW YORK

SALOME

A TRAGEDY IN ONE ACT

TRANSLATED FROM THE FRENCH OF

OSCAR WILDE

BY LORD ALFRED DOUGLAS

WITH A NEW INTRODUCTION

BY HOLBROOK JACKSON

DECORATED & HAND-ILLUMINATED

BY VALENTI ANGELO

FOR THE HERITAGE PRESS

NEW YORK

DECEMBER 1945

introduction

OSCAR WILDE

introduction

OSCAR WILDE wrote *Salome* at the height of his powers. He had lived down the æsthetic posturings satirised by Gilbert in *Patience,* and was on the eve of a new and more prosperous reputation as a fashionable dramatist. The play was written in 1891, and in that first year of a memorable decade he published no less than four books, each of them a characteristic expression of his own genius and a contribution to the romantic movement of the eighteen-nineties of which he was so distinguished a figure. The books were *The Picture of Dorian Gray, Intentions, Lord Arthur Savile's Crime* and *A House of Pomegranates.* When *Salome* appeared, Wilde had already captivated society with *Lady Windermere's Fan.* He had become a public figure of a different sort: a literary dandy who had revived some of the splendour of the Regency, a wit whose sayings were current in Mayfair as well as in Chelsea, and a playwright of more than usual promise. Yet *Salome,* one of his greatest works, missed fire. Instead of being received as a serious work of art it met with contempt, anger and abuse.

Few plays have had a more remarkable history. It was written in French, and published simultaneously in Paris and London in 1893, unillustrated save for a small device by Felicien Rops. It was translated into English, and published in London and Boston in the following year, with a cover-design and twelve illustrations by Aubrey Beardsley. It is a skilfully constructed stage-play, and although, on its author's admission, it was not composed for the theatre, it has been played successfully all over the world. It also formed the basis of an opera for Richard Strauss, and its chief incident, Salome dancing with the head of John the Baptist, was a popular feature in the repertory of Maud Allan. Many believed, in spite of Wilde's denials, that the play was written for Sarah Bernhardt, but whether that was the high objective of the dramatist or not, *Salome* impressed the great actress so much when Wilde read the manuscript to her, at the house of Henry Irving, that she put it in rehearsal at the Palace Theatre, London, a year before it was published, intending to produce it immediately with herself in the title rôle. Her design was frustrated by the Lord Chamberlain, who banned the play under a law, still in force, which forbids the dramatisation of scriptural subjects on the English stage. Wilde was furious when he learnt that he was to be robbed of the satisfaction of hearing, as he said, 'the greatest tragic actress of any stage' lend to his prose 'the music of her flute-like voice'. In his disappointment he threatened to become a French subject and Sarah Bernhardt consoled him by promising to produce the play at the Porte St. Martin, her own theatre in Paris. But neither his threat nor her promise was carried out, and the honour of giving *Salome* its first performance goes to Lugné-Poë, who presented it to the playgoers of Paris at the Théâtre de L'Oeuvre in 1896. Oscar Wilde, who was enduring the first year of his imprisonment, tasted, in Reading Gaol, the bitter-sweet of something like posthumous fame when his adored Paris gave the play hospitality while London was smugly forgetting his work and apologising for his fame. In 1901, within a year after Wilde's death, it was produced in Berlin and had a regular place on the German stage up to 1914. Five years were to pass before England saw a production of the play, and then it was a private performance given by the New Stage Club with Robert Farquharson as Herod. In the following year it was produced again privately, by the Literary Theatre Society, with scenery by Charles Ricketts, whose genius for design, which Wilde was one of the first to recognise and encourage, had some years earlier added typographical distinction to *A House of Pomegranates* and *The Sphinx.*

Yet *Salome,* which Lord Alfred Douglas translated into English, Aubrey Beardsley illustrated, Richard Strauss set to music, Sarah Bernhardt desired to produce, and Charles Ricketts decorated for the stage: this play which has been performed in all the capitals of the western world more constantly than any other modern English play, and which, furthermore, has been paid the compliment of translation into thirteen languages, has aroused suspicion among English and American critics and been condemned by them as degenerate, blasphemous or unactable. Such an anomaly deserves examination.

I

It has been said that *Salome* suffered for the sins of Aubrey Beardsley, its first illustrator. That may be hard to believe today, but in the early nineties Beardsley, not Wilde, was regarded as the typical exponent of decadent art. Wilde was a fashionable jester, and like the court jester of old he was privileged to juggle with conventional opinions. He played his part so wittily and with such good humour that the Philistines whom he prodded became his main supporters, much as Bernard Shaw has raised laughter when he intended to raise howls. Beardsley's method of satire permitted no such tolerance. His drawings were not popularly understood, and it was felt that there was something sinister about them. Like Wilde and Shaw, Beardsley delighted to shock the middle classes, not, however, for the good of their souls, but because he disliked their tastes and habits. His gibes lacked playfulness, and suffered from a solemn naughtiness which favoured the use of obstetrical and phallic 'properties' when it was not underlining the perversities in the dialogue. It was probably the essential seriousness of his drawings as much as

their impudence which aroused opposition and prejudiced the reception of the play.

It is said, also, that there was an underlying hostility between Beardsley and Wilde which was reflected in the illustrations to the play. Such conclusions are more readily inferred than proved. Some of the illustrations, it is true, appear to be ironical comments upon the theme of the play and its treatment. Wilde, who was as amiable as he was vain, did not seem to object, possibly because he was a showman as well as an artist, and recognised the advantage of having his play discussed, even a little contemptuously, by the most discussed artist of the moment. So Herod, Herodias, and even the Moon, which plays a leading part in the drama, were allowed to appear with some of the author's features; but when Beardsley amused himself by insinuating obscure symbols into his designs, with the lewd relish of a boy who scribbles bawdry on a wall, there were objections, though whether from Wilde or his publishers, or both, has not been revealed. At any rate there was considerable bowdlerizing of the more daring drawings, and some were suppressed at first but appeared in later editions.

On the other hand there is one piece of evidence that Wilde thought well of the illustrations. It occurs in a letter addressed to Mrs. Patrick Campbell during a performance of The Second Mrs. Tanqueray carrying a request that the interpreter of Paula Tanqueray should permit 'a very brilliant and wonderful young artist' to pay his compliments to her. He has just, Wilde wrote, 'from the row where he and Beardsley sat 'illustrated my play Salome for me, and has a copy of the edition de luxe which he wishes to lay at your feet. His drawings are quite wonderful.' The tone of this letter removes any doubt of Wilde not being gratified by his association with Beardsley.

There was certainly some incompatibility between the collaborators, for at a time when Wilde was an established romantic Beardsley was becoming progressively classical; he had passed from the romanticism of the illustrations to the Morte d'Arthur and was borrowing from Japan a new art of distinct formal expression which was finally achieved in the classical severity of the designs for the Rape of the Lock. These differences are summed up in a scrap of conversation. Beardsley was extolling his new-found love of Pope. 'Ah,' said Wilde, 'there are two ways of disliking poetry. One is to dislike it, and the other is to like Pope.' Beardsley's distaste for Wilde in this state may have been increased also by a circumstance not generally known. Salome had been translated into English by Lord Alfred Douglas, at Wilde's request. But the translation does not appear to have given satisfaction, and Wilde either encouraged Beardsley to try his hand at it, or, as Lord Alfred Douglas says, 'yielded to the solicitation of Aubrey Beardsley, who declared that he could do a splendid translation, and that he thoroughly understood the spirit of the play.' The reason, however, was so little to Wilde's liking, that he their impudence which aroused opposition and prejudiced the reception of the play.

It is said, also, that there was an underlying hostility between Beardsley and Wilde which was reflected in the illustrations to the play. Such conclusions are more readily inferred than proved. Some of the illustrations, it is true, appear to be ironical comments upon the theme of the play and its treatment. Wilde, who was as amiable as he was vain, did not seem to object, possibly because he was a showman as well as an artist, and recognised the advantage of having his play decorated, even a little outrageously, by the most discussed artist of the moment. So Herod, Herodias, and even the Moon, which plays a leading part in the drama, were allowed to appear with some of the author's features; but when Beardsley amused himself by insinuating phallic symbols into his designs with the lewd relish of a boy who scribbles bawdry on a wall there were objections, though whether from Wilde or his publishers, or both, has not been revealed. At any rate, there was considerable bowdlerizing of the more daring drawings, and some were suppressed at first but appeared in later editions.

On the other hand there is one piece of evidence that Wilde thought well of the illustrations. It occurs in a letter addressed to Mrs. Patrick Campbell during a performance of *The Second Mrs. Tanqueray,* carrying a request that the interpreter of Paula Tanqueray should permit 'a very brilliant and wonderful young artist' to 'bow his compliments' to her. 'He has just,' Wilde wrote, from the box where he and Beardsley sat, 'illustrated my play *Salome* for me, and has a copy of the *edition de luxe* which he wishes to lay at your feet. His drawings are quite wonderful'. The tone of this letter removes any doubt of Wilde not being gratified by his association with Beardsley.

There was certainly some incompatibility between the collaborators, for at a time when Wilde was an unabashed romantic Beardsley was becoming progressively classical; he had passed from the romanticism of the illustrations to the *Morte d'Arthur* and was borrowing from Japanese art a desired formal expression which was finally achieved in the classical serenity of the designs for the *Rape of the Lock.* These differences are summed up in a scrap of conversation. Beardsley was extolling his new-found love of Pope: 'Ah,' said Wilde, 'there are two ways of disliking poetry. One is to dislike it, and the other is to like Pope'. Beardsley's distaste for Wilde at this time may have been increased also by a circumstance not generally known. *Salome* had been translated into English by Lord Alfred Douglas, at Wilde's request. But the translation does not appear to have given satisfaction, and Wilde either encouraged Beardsley to try his hand at it, or, as Lord Alfred Douglas says, 'yielded to the solicitation of Aubrey Beardsley, who declared that he could do a splendid translation, and that he thoroughly understood the spirit of the play'. The result, however, was so little to Wilde's liking that he

[6]

refused to use it, and reverted to the translation made by Lord Alfred Douglas.

After Wilde's downfall Beardsley's resentment deepened, and we find him agreeing to draw for a new periodical projected by Leonard Smithers only if 'Oscar Wilde contributes nothing...anonymously, pseudonymously or otherwise'. It may be presumed that this attitude was aggravated by professional fears. Those fears were not groundless, for the revulsion of feeling brought about by the downfall of Wilde robbed Beardsley of a considerable portion of his means of livelihood. The breach thus widened was never closed, although in the last year of his life Beardsley was so impressed by *The Ballad of Reading Gaol* that he 'promised at once to do a frontispiece for it' but, adds Smithers, in a letter to Wilde, 'in a manner which immediately convinced me that he will never do it'. It is more charitable to think that his failure to do so was through ill-health, not ill-will. Beardsley evidently was conscious that the *Salome* drawings were in doubtful taste. Yet, in his final repentant mood, when he was beginning to regret the artistic indiscretions of his youth, he told the poet, Father John Gray, author of *Silverpoints,* who had received him into the Roman Catholic faith, that he in no way regretted his pictures to *Salome.* It is not clear if this was an attempt to justify the more facetious of those pictorial comments, or whether he still delighted in his snooks at Wilde.

II

It is not surprising that so unusual a play has received abundance of both praise and blame, or even, as it happens, more blame than praise, and it is worth remark that many who liked it praised grudgingly, as though with a guilty conscience. The play, in the first place, was sufficiently novel in theme and treatment to arouse all the usual antipathies for what is new and strange; in the second, it had provoked suspicion because it had been censored. This particular suspicion was illogical for, as Wilde pointed out, biblical themes might and did appear on the English stage if set to music. In the third place, it was labelled morbid and decadent at a time when those words were loosely used as synonyms for immoral. Its exotic characteristics were an easy mark for the righteous indignation aroused by the trial and downfall of Wilde, and nothing could exceed the vituperation of the earliest reviewers, one of whom, in *The Times,* was comparatively moderate when he described the play as 'an arrangement in blood and ferocity, morbid, bizarre, repulsive, and very often offensive in its adaptation of scriptural phraseology to situations the reverse of sacred'.

It is quite possible for a play to be simultaneously an expression of genius and of degeneracy. But English-speaking critics of many years ago were so busily engaged in denying artistry to what was believed to be immoral that they overlooked the resemblance of the play, in at

[7]

less sense of its aspects, to the morality drama of the middle ages.
Salome is among other things a morality play, and although it contains
little virtue to be rewarded, vice is thought to be had an end that the
most exacting moralist ought to be gratified. Not, however, a morality
in the manner of medieval folk drama, but a modern variety into which
the soul with all its maladies has crept, a tragedy of spiritual disharmony. Each character founders through lack of balance between
body and soul. There is nothing new here, for although Wilde boasted
of his adherence to art for art's sake, he was constitutionally didactic.
The Preface to Dorian Gray, which caused so much irritation, may be
the disguise of a repressed moralist, which peeps out in such sayings as
'the moral life of man forms part of the subject-matter of the artist, but
the morality of art consists in the perfect use of an imperfect medium'.
Moral problems are discussed or implied in most of his works, and his
didacticism reaches its fullest expression in the Prose Poem, the Ballad
of Reading Gaol and De Profundis. When Dorian Gray was attacked for
its wickedness, Wilde pointed out that it was 'a story with a moral',
the moral being 'All excess, as well as all renunciation, brings its own
punishment', in a characteristic anticlimax he adds: 'Is this an error? I
fear it is. It is the only error in the book'. He might have made the
same claim for Salome—and the same riposte.

III

In so far as Salome is decadent, it is in the mood, in the attitude, rather
than the treatment, that is. If decadence has a precise meaning. The
theme in itself is unpleasant, but not necessarily degenerate, and its un-
cleanness is not the dramatist's fault, whatever may have prompted
him to choose it as a subject. It would be rash to diagnose degeneracy
in an artist even when he chooses a degenerate theme. The Prince of
Denmark may be decadent, but not Shakespeare. The Princess of Judea
is obviously degenerate but that is not evidence against Oscar Wilde.

IV

There are several ways of approaching this remarkable work. Probably Wilde intended it as a prose-poem, an Oriental tale, a type of, deliberately ornate, sensuous, excessive, glittering with words and phrases
as foreign as or his hummingbirds or opals, a tropical interlude in
the cool plain-tune of English letters. Or you may take it as a mannered dialogue à la Maeterlinck, a sub-tropical Pelléas and Mélisande, a
fantastic conversation-piece for marionettes with magic tugging and
passionate smoke in place of quiet talk. You may even enjoy it as a
brilliant melodrama, or it may even provide you with a profitable excursion into the realms of Freudian psychology. Few plays are so accommodating, and its possible they are not even then exhausted. The ingenious reader may discover others for himself, but I must mention at

least some of its aspects, to the morality drama of the middle ages. *Salome* is, among other things, a morality play, and although it contains little virtue to be rewarded, vice is brought to so bad an end that the most exacting moralist ought to be gratified. Not, however, a 'morality' in the manner of medieval folk drama, but a modern variety into which 'the soul with all its maladies' has crept: a tragedy of spiritual disharmony. Each character founders through lack of balance between body and soul. There is nothing new here, for although Wilde boasted of his adherence to art for art's sake, he was constitutionally didactic. The Preface to *Dorian Gray,* which caused so much irritation, may be the disguise of a repressed moralist, which peeps out in such sayings as 'the moral life of man forms part of the subject-matter of the artist, but the morality of art consists in the perfect use of an imperfect medium'. Moral problems are discussed or implied in most of his works, and his didacticism reaches its fullest expression in the *Prose Poems,* the *Ballad of Reading Gaol* and *De Profundis.* When *Dorian Gray* was attacked for its 'wickedness' Wilde pointed out that it was 'a story with a moral', the moral being: 'All excess, as well as all renunciation, brings its own punishment'. In a characteristic anticlimax he adds: 'Is this an error? I fear it is. It is the only error in the book'. He might have made the same claim for *Salome*—and the same riposte.

III

In so far as *Salome* is decadent, it is in the mood, in the attitude, rather than the treatment, that is if decadence has a precise meaning. The theme in itself is unpleasant, but not necessarily degenerate, and its unpleasantness is not the dramatist's fault, whatever may have prompted him to choose it as a subject. It would be rash to diagnose degeneracy in an artist even when he chooses a degenerate theme. The Prince of Denmark may be decadent, but not Shakespeare. The Princess of Judæa is obviously degenerate, but that is not evidence against Oscar Wilde.

IV

There are several ways of approaching this remarkable work. Probably Wilde intended it as a prose-poem, an Oscarian *jeu d'esprit,* deliberately ornate, sensuous, excessive, glittering with words and phrases as foreign as orchids, humming-birds or opals: a tropical interlude in the cool pleasaunces of English letters. Or you may take it as a mannered dialogue *à la Maeterlinck,* a sub-tropical *Pelléas and Melisande:* a fantastic conversation piece for marionettes with tragic nagging and passionate shrieks in place of quiet talk. You may again enjoy it as a brilliant melodrama: or it may even provide you with a profitable excursion into the realms of Freudian psychology. Few plays are so accommodating, and its possibilities are not even then exhausted. The ingenious reader may discover others for himself, but I must mention at least one more. *Salome* is a godsend to those who enjoy tracing origins. Oscar Wilde offers more opportunities for the excitements of literary research than any poet since Wharton and Warburton explored the backwoods of Milton and Pope.

The legend of Salome was no novelty when Wilde took it up. It had been the theme of imaginative works by Flaubert, Huysmans and Jules Laforgue, with which he must have been familiar. I have already hinted at the resemblance between the style of *Salome* and the earlier plays of Maeterlinck which treated human beings as though they were fate-led puppets. The resemblance occurs in the shorter passages which form such an effective contrast to the gradually lengthening speeches of the climax. A throw-back to Flaubert's *Temptation of St. Anthony* is also probable, and the Bible, particularly the *Song of Songs,* must not be over-looked when the sources of Wilde's cadences are being considered. The origins of the story provide one or two problems of interest, notably Wilde's confusion of Herod Antipas with Herod the Great and Herod Agrippa. Commentators have wondered whether this was intentional in the medieval manner of romancing, which is probable, or the result of ignorance or carelessness which, in an artist of Wilde's integrity, is unlikely.

There is adventure also in an examination of the French in which Wilde wrote the play and the English into which Lord Alfred Douglas translated it. It has been said that Wilde's French, though correct, is not that of a Frenchman. But no less an authority than André Gide has writ-ten that Wilde knew French almost perfectly and in speaking it had scarcely any accent. Defects of accent, in any case, could not trouble his written French, and other irregularities would be erased by French friends to whom he could have submitted, and actually did submit, the manuscript. Nor must we under-estimate his admitted knowledge of French and familiarity with French literature. France was Oscar Wilde's spiritual home. 'I adore Paris,' he told a representative of *Le Gaulois,* when *Salome* had been censored, 'I also adore your language. To me there are only two languages in the world: French and Greek'. Long before then he had been a regular visitor to France, an associate of French men of letters, and for some time he became a Parisian with headquarters at the Hotel Voltaire, where he is said to have posed as a latter-day Balzac. He achieved fame as a wit, an Irish Barbey d'Aurevilly or Gerard de Nerval, in the cafés of the boulevards before his brilliance dazzled the dinner-tables of the West End of London.

It could be argued that Wilde plunged into French out of conceit. But however much of a *tour de force Salome* may have been, or whatever the immediate motive of its composition in a foreign language, it was no merely irresponsible enterprise. The explanation given by Wilde in an interview when the play was facing the first antagonism it aroused bears the mark of sincerity. 'My idea of writing the play was simply

this,' he said, 'I have one instrument that I know I can command, and that is the English language. There was another instrument to which I had listened all my life, and I wanted once to touch this new instrument to see whether I could make any beautiful thing out of it.' That is the spirit of adventure—but not of a mere adventurer. Wilde knew that an Englishman who has learnt French could never write it as it would be written by a Frenchman. But a foreigner's French may have merits of its own. 'The play was written in Paris,' he continued, 'where I read it to some young poets who admired it immensely. Of course there are modes of expression that a French man of letters would not have used, but they give a certain relief or colour to the play. A great deal of the curious effect that Maeterlinck produced comes from the fact that he, a Flamand by race, writes in an alien language. The same thing is true of Rossetti, who, although he wrote in English, was essentially Latin in temperament'. We know also that before going to press the play was submitted to Marcel Schwob, the French friend to whom Wilde dedicated *The Sphinx*. Schwob is believed to have made three corrections, and later told Robert Ross that the character and spontaneity of the style would have been spoiled if he had 'tried to harmonise it with the diction demanded by the French Academy'. In addition to that, it is probable that the manuscript was read by another friend, Pierre Louys, to whom the French version was dedicated. It is rumoured also that the work benefited from the criticism of André Gide; but that is disputed by Lord Alfred Douglas with the support of Robert Harborough Sherard who asserts, on the authority of Marcel Schwob, that neither Gide nor Louÿs played any part in the business.

V

The English can be judged more easily by comparison with Wilde's normal style and the result is a victory for the translator, whoever he was, and there is still some doubt. Aubrey Beardsley can, of course, be ruled out. The remaining possible translators are Lord Alfred Douglas and Wilde himself, or a combination of the two. There can be no doubt that Lord Alfred Douglas made a translation which did not satisfy Wilde. The evidence for this dissatisfaction is in a written statement by Wilde, and his flirtation with the idea of making Beardsley his translator. The translation as originally published (posthumous editions were altered, presumably by Robert Ross) is twice attributed by Oscar Wilde to Lord Alfred Douglas, once in the Dedication: 'To My Friend Lord Alfred Bruce Douglas the Translator of My Play', and again in *De Profundis* where he complains that his masterpiece was spoiled by the translator. It could be argued that the dedication was a compliment to his friend for the trouble he had taken in making a translation which had been rejected or largely re-written, and that the complaint in the famous letter, written in Reading Gaol, and published with the title of

De Profundis, might have been distorted by the sense of grievance from which Wilde was then suffering.

It has always been a puzzle why so self-sufficient a writer did not make his own translation. Lord Alfred Douglas, in the 1931 edition of his *Autobiography,* throws some light on the problem, and incidentally makes it clear that the translation published in 1894, although attributed to him in the dedication, was either solely the work of Wilde, or so altered as to be unrecognisable from his own version. If it is true, as Lord Alfred Douglas asserts, that the play was originally written in English, translated into French, and then re-translated 'more or less' into Wilde's 'own original language', the puzzle is solved, although the circumlocutory way of going about so simple a business still remains a mystery. The close resemblance of the style of the 'translation' to that of Wilde's normal style is also explained.

It was not the mere rendering of words from one language to another that was required. The French of the original is so simple and direct that a literal translation was almost inevitable. The difficulty was with texture and cadence. *Salome* was translated out of a foreign language into the normal language of an author whose style was known and had to be reproduced. Translation would thus become creation. Wilde's style has been reproduced successfully even to its characteristic echoes of other writers, not only Maeterlinck and Flaubert, but Pater, and more surprisingly John Bright, whose image of the beating of the wings of death on the eve of the Crimean War seems to serve Herod as a sign of his own foreboding. In these circumstances it is safe to assume that the English version of the play is largely if not entirely Wilde's.

VI

Salome reveals Wilde's sensitiveness to the behaviour of words. In his most characteristic work words and phrases are given undue prominence. It was a trick caught to some extent from the French Romantics. But it was more than the search for the *mot juste,* a vogue which he first popularised in England. He thought of himself primarily as a lord of language. His love of words was like a painter's love of light, and he tried, as Rossetti had tried before him, to make words do a painter's job. Many of his most elaborate patterns are carefully managed colour schemes. When he first met André Gide he said to him, approvingly, 'You hear with your eyes'. He could have said the same even more truly of himself. He wrote as much for the eye as the ear, in spite of an opinion in *The Critic as Artist* that 'pure art' should please the ear rather than the eye. The look of words and sentences fascinated him. He liked the poise and strut of them. Whatever the importance of his ideas, his writing impresses by memorable words and phrases. The creation of characters was never Wilde's business and rarely his aim, but colour was of first importance in the fantastic palaces he fashioned out of

[11]

words. Words he deliberately selected and arranged so as to give each a curiously self-conscious life in spite of its place in an equally self-conscious pattern. Despite Wilde's preference for words and images which gratify the lust of the eye, *Salome* is a symphony with a colour theme running through. Stripped of its colour it would lose power, and if the work was designed for reading rather than playing it is possible that Wilde used colour for costume and scenery.

Whether that be so or not, the colour motifs are insistent, mannered and often magnificent. They begin at the opening of the play with the description of the scene: a terrace within the Palace of Herod on which is 'an old cistern surrounded by a wall of green bronze'. In the third speech of the play, the Moon is compared to 'a little princess who wears a yellow veil, and whose feet are of silver . . . a princess who has little white doves for feet', and later on to one 'whose eyes are eyes of amber'. Salome is 'the shadow of a white rose in a mirror of silver'. Herodias wears 'a black mitre sewn with pearls' and her hair is 'powdered with blue dust'. Herod drinks three kinds of wine, one 'purple like the cloak of Cæsar', another 'yellow as gold' and the third 'red as blood'. Salome offers Narraboth, the Young Syrian, who dies for love of her, 'a little green flower'.

To Iokanaan, the first Puritan, colour is evil. Herodias to him is the woman 'who saw the images of men painted on the walls, even the images of the Chaldeans painted with colours . . . sent ambassadors into the land of Chaldea', the woman who gave herself up to the Captains of Assyria 'who have baldricks on their loins, and crowns of many colours on their heads' and to the young men of Egypt 'who are clothed in fine linen and hyacinth, whose shields are of gold, whose helmets are of silver . . .'

This colour symphony reaches its height in the contest between Salome and Iokanaan. She is obsessed by the colour of his eyes and mouth. His eyes are 'black holes burned by torches in a tapestry of Tyre. They are like the black caverns where the dragons live . . . black caverns of Egypt in which the dragons make their lairs . . . black lakes troubled by fantastic moons . . .' His body is 'like a thin ivory statue . . . an image of silver . . . a moonbeam . . . a shaft of silver'. Iokanaan recoils from the scrutiny of her 'golden eyes, under her gilded eyelids'. Then the vision of those golden eyes leaps to the climax of a desire which she can only express in colours. In the passages describing Salome's passion for Iokanaan's body Oscar Wilde can be seen deliberately fashioning his colour scheme, placing his colours where he wants them, giving them point and position, sound as well as light.

The first movement is in white:
'I am amorous of thy body, Iokanaan! Thy body is white like the lilies of a field that the mower hath never mowed. Thy body is white like the

snows that lie on the mountains of Judæa, and come down into the valleys. The roses in the garden of the Queen of Arabia are not so white as thy body. Neither the roses of the garden of the Queen of Arabia, the garden of spices of the Queen of Arabia, nor the feet of the dawn when they light on the leaves, nor the breast of the moon when she lies on the breast of the sea . . . There is nothing in the world so white as thy body . . .'

There is an interlude of recoil when she is spurned by the prophet, and the theme becomes black:

'Thy body is hideous . . . It is horrible, thy body is horrible. It is of thy hair that I am enamoured, Iokanaan. Thy hair is like clusters of grapes, like the clusters of black grapes that hang from the vine-trees of Edom in the land of the Edomites. Thy hair is like the cedars of Lebanon, like the great cedars of Lebanon that give their shade to the lions and to the robbers who would hide them by day. The long black nights, when the moon hides her face, when the stars are afraid, are not so black . . . The silence that dwells in the forest is not so black. There is nothing in the world that is so black as thy hair . . .'

The climax of the movement is in the key of red when Salome chants her notorious dithyramb on the lips of Iokanaan:

'Thy hair is horrible . . . I love not thy hair . . . It is thy mouth that I desire, Iokanaan. Thy mouth is like a band of scarlet on a tower of ivory . . . The pomegranate-flowers that blossom in the gardens of Tyre, and are redder than roses, are not so red. The red blasts of trumpets that herald the approach of kings, and make afraid the enemy, are not so red. Thy mouth is redder than the feet of . . . the doves who inhabit the temples and are fed by the priests. It is redder than the feet of him who cometh from a forest where he hath slain a lion, and seen gilded tigers. Thy mouth is like a branch of coral that fishers have found in the twilight of the sea, the coral that they keep for the kings! . . . It is like the vermilion that the Moabites find in the mines of Moab, the vermilion that the kings take from them. It is like the bow of the King of the Persians, that is painted with vermilion, and is tipped with coral. There is nothing in the world that is so red as thy mouth . . .'

And with these words the symphony of colour may be said to end; but *Salome* is not only symphonic in its coloration. Wilde's use of words is consciously musical. His rhythms and repetitions of phrases follow a musical technique. It is no wonder that the play has attracted musicians, and it is significant that Richard Strauss did not find it necessary to depart materially from the words of the play.

VII

The critics have not even been able to agree about the play's stage-worthiness. It has been called dialogue rather than drama, and some have thought it unplayable. That in Wilde's opinion was no defect. In an address to the Playgoers' Club, a year before *Salome* was published, and probably with *Salome* in mind, he described drama as 'the art of making people express themselves in dialogue ... The stage is only a frame furnished with a set of puppets. It is to the play no more than a picture frame is to a painting.... The present decadence of the English stage is due to the fact that the actor, the instrumentalist, the medium, has become more important than the creative actor or dramatist. The present has given us two English plays—*The Cenci* and *Atalanta in Calydon*. Neither was actable.' Whether written for presentation or not, *Salome* has more cohesion, more stage-sense than any of his comedies, except perhaps the best of them, *The Importance of Being Earnest,* and even in that amusing piece the stage carpenter is often more in evidence than the dramatist.

I have not seen *Salome* played, so cannot express an opinion upon its theatrical qualities, but it is known to have had a successful theatrical career for the better part of forty years. It was believed at one time that the long speeches towards the end were unactable. But that has never been the opinion of actors. Indeed it was Sarah Bernhardt who first saw its theatrical possibilities, and the long, and for a long time continuous, record of production can do nothing but support her opinion. It may be true, as Robert Ross believed, that 'with his keen sense of the theatre' Wilde 'would never have consented to the long speech of Salome at the end in a drama intended for the stage, even in the days of long speeches'. That is no proof that Salome's long speech, however difficult, is impossible. Max Beerbohm, with his invariable insight, recognises Wilde's 'mastery in his handling of this slow and simple form of tragedy—a form compounded, seemingly, of Sophocles and Maeterlinck in even proportions'; and he agrees that technically it is a good stage-play, but 'not a good play for the stage' because it is 'too horrible for definite and corporeal presentment'. In an uneasy and more recent criticism Arthur Symons, whilst being moved by the 'strange fascination' of the play, will not admit that it is a success. It is a dialogue and 'cannot be designated drama'. It is 'a series of poses' and 'on the stage these poses are less decorative than on the page'. The poses are 'languid, horrible and frozen', and Salome is a soulless doll 'set in motion by some pitiless destiny, personified momentarily by her mother: Herod is a nodding Mandarin in a Chinese grotesque'. The play itself is 'a sort of celebration of dark rites'.

But whether the play is playable or not is of little moment to the reader. Lord Alfred Douglas, when still an undergraduate at Oxford, was of the opinion that *Salome* would lose rather than gain by performance. 'To be appreciated', he wrote, 'it must be abstracted, and to be abstracted it must be read'. Most readers will admit that the reading of *Salome* is an experience which impresses itself upon the mind and stirs the imagination. The size of the play helps. It has only one act and can thus be 'abstracted' and absorbed easily. The slow movement makes it inevitable that incidents and persons, vivid in themselves, should become more vivid, should be more deeply etched upon the memory by the simple yet subtle repetition of words and cadences which linger in the mind like fragments of music. The expression of a tragic theme by the play of words, by the use of words as a composer of music uses tones, is unique in English drama; but of equal distinction is the coordination of the movement into a crescendo which develops with grim fatality to the murder of Iokanaan and of Salome dancing with his head and kissing his dead lips:

'Ah, I have kissed thy mouth, Iokanaan, I have kissed thy mouth. There was a bitter taste on thy lips. Was it the taste of blood? ... But perchance it was the taste of love...'

And when the horror of the thing becomes unbearable Wilde brings relief with a masterly climax. The stage is almost dark: suddenly a moonbeam falls on Salome covering her with light. Herod sees her. 'Kill that woman!' he yells, and the soldiers rush forward and crush beneath their shields Salome, daughter of Herodias, Princess of Judæa.

VIII

The test of such a work, as of all works of fiction, dramatic or narrative, is not whether it is wise or unwise, moral or immoral, but whether its parts chime harmoniously together. Feelings may rebel against the theme, but that, if an objection at all and not the result of mere prejudice or undue queasiness, concerns the subject and not the artistry which has given it form. If it were otherwise much of what is most distinctive in classical as well as modern drama and fiction would be condemned. There are, of course, limits to the objectionable, but the frontiers of nastiness and tragedy are wide apart. It is largely a matter of technique. Art purifies all subjects, not by idealising them but by showing them in their true relation to life. The artist achieves that result more by technique than by theme. It is one of the functions of art to quell the rebellious feelings of the perceiver by transferring them and him to the realm of the imagination. When the imagination rebels it is time to doubt the authenticity of a work of art. For the rest it is the business of a critic (and every reader is a critic) to look at a work of art, a play in this instance, with, as far as possible, no preconceptions about its author, and to consider only what he finds there.

HOLBROOK JACKSON

[15]

SALOMÉ

SCENE—A great terrace in the Palace of Herod, set above the banqueting hall. Some soldiers are leaning over the balcony. To the right there is a gigantic staircase, to the left, at the back, an old cistern surrounded by a wall of green bronze. The moon is shining very brightly.

THE YOUNG SYRIAN
How beautiful is the Princess Salome to-night!

THE PAGE OF HERODIAS
Look at the moon. How strange the moon seems! She is like a woman rising from a tomb. She is like a dead woman. One might fancy she was looking for dead things.

THE YOUNG SYRIAN
She has a strange look. She is like a little princess who wears a yellow veil, and whose feet are of silver. She is like a princess who has little white doves for feet. One might fancy she was dancing.

THE PAGE OF HERODIAS
She is like a woman who is dead. She moves very slowly.

[Noise in the banqueting-hall.]

FIRST SOLDIER
What an uproar! Who are those wild beasts howling?

SECOND SOLDIER
The Jews. They are always like that. They are disputing about their religion.

FIRST SOLDIER
Why do they dispute about their religion?

SECOND SOLDIER
I cannot tell. They are always doing it. The Pharisees, for instance, say that there are angels, and the Sadducees declare that angels do not exist.

FIRST SOLDIER
I think it is ridiculous to dispute about such things.

THE YOUNG SYRIAN
How beautiful is the Princess Salome to-night!

THE PAGE OF HERODIAS
You are always looking at her. You look at her too much. It is dangerous to look at people in such fashion. Something terrible may happen.

THE YOUNG SYRIAN
She is very beautiful to-night.

salome

SCENE. *A great terrace in the Palace of Herod, set above the banqueting-hall. Some soldiers are leaning over the balcony. To the right there is a gigantic staircase; to the left, at the back, an old cistern surrounded by a wall of green bronze. The moon is shining very brightly.*

THE YOUNG SYRIAN
How beautiful is the Princess Salome to-night!

THE PAGE OF HERODIAS
Look at the moon. How strange the moon seems! She is like a woman rising from a tomb. She is like a dead woman. One might fancy she was looking for dead things.

THE YOUNG SYRIAN
She has a strange look. She is like a little princess who wears a yellow veil, and whose feet are of silver. She is like a princess who has little white doves for feet. One might fancy she was dancing.

THE PAGE OF HERODIAS
She is like a woman who is dead. She moves very slowly.

[*Noise in the banqueting-hall.*]

FIRST SOLDIER
What an uproar! Who are those wild beasts howling?

SECOND SOLDIER
The Jews. They are always like that. They are disputing about their religion.

FIRST SOLDIER
Why do they dispute about their religion?

SECOND SOLDIER
I cannot tell. They are always doing it. The Pharisees, for instance, say that there are angels, and the Sadducees declare that angels do not exist.

FIRST SOLDIER
I think it is ridiculous to dispute about such things.

THE YOUNG SYRIAN
How beautiful is the Princess Salome to-night!

THE PAGE OF HERODIAS
You are always looking at her. You look at her too much. It is dangerous to look at people in such fashion. Something terrible may happen.

THE YOUNG SYRIAN
She is very beautiful to-night.

FIRST SOLDIER

The Tetrarch has a sombre aspect.

SECOND SOLDIER

Yes; he has a sombre aspect.

FIRST SOLDIER

He is looking at something.

SECOND SOLDIER

He is looking at some one.

FIRST SOLDIER

At whom is he looking?

SECOND SOLDIER

I cannot tell.

THE YOUNG SYRIAN

How pale the Princess is! Never have I seen her so pale. She is like the shadow of a white rose in a mirror of silver.

THE PAGE OF HERODIAS

You must not look at her. You look too much at her.

FIRST SOLDIER

Herodias has filled the cup of the Tetrarch.

THE CAPPADOCIAN

Is that the Queen Herodias, she who wears a black mitre sewed with pearls, and whose hair is powdered with blue dust?

FIRST SOLDIER

Yes; that is Herodias, the Tetrarch's wife.

SECOND SOLDIER

The Tetrarch is very fond of wine. He has wine of three sorts. One which is brought from the Island of Samothrace, and is purple like the cloak of Cæsar.

THE CAPPADOCIAN

I have never seen Cæsar.

SECOND SOLDIER

Another that comes from a town called Cyprus, and is as yellow as gold.

THE CAPPADOCIAN

I love gold.

SECOND SOLDIER

And the third is a wine of Sicily. That wine is as red as blood.

THE NUBIAN

The gods of my country are very fond of blood. Twice in the year we sacrifice to them young men and maidens: fifty young men and a hundred maidens. But I am afraid that we never give them quite enough, for they are very harsh to us.

THE CAPPADOCIAN

In my country there are no gods left. The Romans have driven them out. There are some who say that they have hidden them-

selves in the mountains, but I do not believe it. Three nights I have been on the mountains seeking them everywhere. I did not find them, and at last I called them by their names, and they did not come. I think they are dead.

FIRST SOLDIER

The Jews worship a God that one cannot see.

THE CAPPADOCIAN

I cannot understand that.

FIRST SOLDIER

In fact they only believe in things that one cannot see.

THE CAPPADOCIAN

That seems to me altogether ridiculous.

THE VOICE OF IOKANAAN

After me shall come another mightier than I. I am not worthy so much as to unloose the latchet of his shoes. When he cometh the solitary places shall be glad. They shall blossom like the rose. The eyes of the blind shall see the day, and the ears of the deaf shall be opened. The sucking child shall put his hand upon the dragon's lair, he shall lead the lions by their manes.

SECOND SOLDIER

Make him be silent. He is always saying ridiculous things.

FIRST SOLDIER

No, no. He is a holy man. He is very gentle, too. Every day when I give him to eat he thanks me.

THE CAPPADOCIAN

Who is he?

FIRST SOLDIER

A prophet.

THE CAPPADOCIAN

What is his name?

FIRST SOLDIER

Iokanaan.

THE CAPPADOCIAN

Whence comes he?

FIRST SOLDIER

From the desert, where he fed on locusts and wild honey. He was clothed in camel's hair, and round his loins he had a leathern belt. He was very terrible to look upon. A great multitude used to follow him. He even had disciples.

THE CAPPADOCIAN

What is he talking of?

FIRST SOLDIER

We can never tell. Sometimes he says things that affright one, but it is impossible to understand what he says.

THE CAPPADOCIAN

May one see him?

FIRST SOLDIER

No. The Tetrarch has forbidden it.

THE YOUNG SYRIAN

The Princess has hidden her face behind her fan! Her little white hands are fluttering like doves that fly to their dove-cots. They are like white butterflies. They are just like white butterflies.

THE PAGE OF HERODIAS

What is that to you? Why do you look at her? You must not look at her. . . . Something terrible may happen.

THE CAPPADOCIAN

[*Pointing to the cistern.*] What a strange prison!

SECOND SOLDIER

It is an old cistern.

THE CAPPADOCIAN

An old cistern! That must be a poisonous place in which to dwell!

SECOND SOLDIER

Oh no! For instance, the Tetrarch's brother, his elder brother, the first husband of Herodias the Queen, was imprisoned there for twelve years. It did not kill him. At the end of the twelve years he had to be strangled.

THE CAPPADOCIAN

Strangled? Who dared to do that?

SECOND SOLDIER

[*Pointing to the Executioner, a huge negro.*] That man yonder, Naaman.

THE CAPPADOCIAN

He was not afraid?

SECOND SOLDIER

Oh no! The Tetrarch sent him the ring.

THE CAPPADOCIAN

What ring?

SECOND SOLDIER

The death ring. So he was not afraid.

THE CAPPADOCIAN

Yet it is a terrible thing to strangle a king.

FIRST SOLDIER

Why? Kings have but one neck, like other folk.

THE CAPPADOCIAN

I think it terrible.

THE YOUNG SYRIAN

The Princess is getting up! She is leaving the table! She looks very troubled. Ah, she is coming this way. Yes, she is coming towards us. How pale she is! Never have I seen her so pale.

THE PAGE OF HERODIAS

Do not look at her. I pray you not to look at her.

THE YOUNG SYRIAN

She is like a dove that has strayed. . . . She is like a narcissus

FIRST SOLDIER

No. The Tetrarch has forbidden it.

THE PAGE OF HERODIAS

The Princess has hidden her face behind her fan! Her little white hands are fluttering like doves that fly to their dove-cots. They are like white butterflies. They are just like butterflies.

THE VOICE OF JOKANAAN

What is that to you? Why do you look at her? You must not look at her. ... Something terrible may happen.

THE CAPPADOCIAN

(Pointing to the cistern.) What a strange prison!

SECOND SOLDIER

It is an old cistern.

THE CAPPADOCIAN

An old cistern! That must be a poisonous place in which to dwell.

SECOND SOLDIER

Oh no! For instance, the Tetrarch's brother, his elder brother, the first husband of Herodias the Queen, was imprisoned there for twelve years. It did not kill him. At the end of the twelve years he had to be strangled.

THE CAPPADOCIAN

Strangled? Who dared to do that?

SECOND SOLDIER

(Pointing to the Executioner, a huge negro.) That man yonder, Naaman.

THE CAPPADOCIAN

He was not afraid?

SECOND SOLDIER

Oh no! The Tetrarch sent him the ring.

THE CAPPADOCIAN

What ring?

SECOND SOLDIER

The death ring. So he was not afraid.

THE CAPPADOCIAN

Yet it is a terrible thing to strangle a king.

FIRST SOLDIER

Why? Kings have but one neck, like other folk.

THE CAPPADOCIAN

I think it terrible.

THE YOUNG SYRIAN

The Princess is getting up! She is leaving the table! She looks very troubled. Ah, she is coming this way. Yes, she is coming towards us. How pale she is! Never have I seen her so pale.

THE PAGE OF HERODIAS

Do not look at her. I pray you not to look at her.

THE YOUNG SYRIAN

She is like a dove that has strayed. ... She is like a narcissus trembling in the wind. . . She is like a silver flower.

[*Enter Salome.*]

SALOME

I will not stay. I cannot stay. Why does the Tetrarch look at me all the while with his mole's eyes under his shaking eyelids? It is strange that the husband of my mother looks at me like that. I know not what it means. Of a truth I know it too well.

THE YOUNG SYRIAN

You have left the feast, Princess?

SALOME

How sweet is the air here! I can breathe here! Within there are Jews from Jerusalem who are tearing each other in pieces over their foolish ceremonies, and barbarians who drink and drink and spill their wine on the pavement, and Greeks from Smyrna with painted eyes and painted cheeks, and frizzed hair curled in columns, and Egyptians silent and subtle, with long nails of jade and russet cloaks, and Romans brutal and coarse, with their uncouth jargon. Ah! how I loathe the Romans! They are rough and common, and they give themselves the airs of noble lords.

THE YOUNG SYRIAN

Will you be seated, Princess.

THE PAGE OF HERODIAS

Why do you speak to her? Oh! something terrible will happen. Why do you look at her?

SALOME

How good to see the moon! She is like a little piece of money, a little silver flower. She is cold and chaste. I am sure she is a virgin. She has the beauty of a virgin. Yes, she is a virgin. She has never defiled herself. She has never abandoned herself to men, like the other goddesses.

THE VOICE OF IOKANAAN

Behold! the Lord hath come. The Son of Man is at hand. The centaurs have hidden themselves in the rivers, and the nymphs have left the rivers, and are lying beneath the leaves in the forests.

SALOME

Who was that who cried out?

SECOND SOLDIER

The prophet, Princess.

SALOME

Ah, the prophet! He of whom the Tetrarch is afraid?

SECOND SOLDIER

We know nothing of that, Princess. It was the prophet Iokanaan who cried out.

THE YOUNG SYRIAN

Is it your pleasure that I bid them bring your litter, Princess?

trembling in the wind.... She is like a silver flower.

[Enter Salome.]

SALOME

I will not stay. I cannot stay. Why does the Tetrarch look at me all the while with his mole's eyes under his shaking eyelids? It is strange that the husband of my mother looks at me like that. I know not what it means. Of a truth I know it too well.

THE YOUNG SYRIAN

You have left the feast, Princess?

SALOME

How sweet is the air here! I can breathe here! Within there are Jews from Jerusalem who are tearing each other in pieces over their foolish ceremonies, and barbarians who drink and drink and spill their wine on the pavement, and Greeks from Smyrna with painted eyes and painted cheeks, and frizzed hair curled in columns, and Egyptians silent and subtle, with long nails of jade and russet cloaks, and Romans brutal and coarse, with their uncouth jargon. Ah! how I loathe the Romans! They are rough and common, and they give themselves the airs of noble lords.

THE YOUNG SYRIAN

Will you be seated, Princess.

THE PAGE OF HERODIAS

Why do you speak to her? Oh! something terrible will happen. Why do you look at her?

SALOME

How good to see the moon! She is like a little piece of money, a little silver flower. She is cold and chaste. I am sure she is a virgin. She has the beauty of a virgin. Yes, she is a virgin. She has never defiled herself. She has never abandoned herself to men, like the other goddesses.

THE VOICE OF IOKANAAN

Behold! the Lord hath come. The Son of Man is at hand. The centaurs have hidden themselves in the rivers, and the nymphs have left the rivers, and are lying beneath the leaves in the forests.

SALOME

Who was that who cried out?

SECOND SOLDIER

The prophet, Princess.

SALOME

Ah, the prophet! He of whom the Tetrarch is afraid?

SECOND SOLDIER

We know nothing of that, Princess. It was the prophet Iokanaan who cried out.

THE YOUNG SYRIAN

Is it your pleasure that I bid them bring your litter, Princess?

The night is fair in the garden.

SALOMÉ

He says terrible things about my mother, does he not?

SECOND SOLDIER

We never understand what he says, Princess.

SALOMÉ

Yes; he says terrible things about her. [Have a Slave]

THE SLAVE

Princess, the Tetrarch prays you to return to the feast.

SALOMÉ

I will not return.

THE YOUNG SYRIAN

Pardon me, Princess, but if you return not some misfortune may happen.

SALOMÉ

Is he an old man, this prophet?

THE YOUNG SYRIAN

Princess, it were better to return. Suffer me to lead you in.

SALOMÉ

This prophet . . . is he an old man?

FIRST SOLDIER

No, Princess, he is quite young.

SECOND SOLDIER

One cannot be sure. There are those who say that he is Elias.

SALOMÉ

Who is Elias?

SECOND SOLDIER

A prophet of this country in bygone days, Princess.

THE SLAVE

What answer may I give the Tetrarch from the Princess?

THE VOICE OF IOKANAAN

Rejoice not, O land of Palestine, because the rod of him who smote thee is broken. For from the seed of the serpent shall come a basilisk, and that which is born of it shall devour the birds.

SALOMÉ

What a strange voice! I would speak with him.

FIRST SOLDIER

I fear it may not be, Princess. The Tetrarch does not suffer any one to speak with him. He has even forbidden the high priest to speak with him.

SALOMÉ

I desire to speak with him.

FIRST SOLDIER

It is impossible, Princess.

The night is fair in the garden.

SALOME

He says terrible things about my mother, does he not?

SECOND SOLDIER

We never understand what he says, Princess.

SALOME

Yes; he says terrible things about her. [*Enter a Slave.*]

THE SLAVE

Princess, the Tetrarch prays you to return to the feast.

SALOME

I will not return.

THE YOUNG SYRIAN

Pardon me, Princess, but if you return not some misfortune may happen.

SALOME

Is he an old man, this prophet?

THE YOUNG SYRIAN

Princess, it were better to return. Suffer me to lead you in.

SALOME

This prophet . . . is he an old man?

FIRST SOLDIER

No, Princess, he is quite young.

SECOND SOLDIER

One cannot be sure. There are those who say that he is Elias.

SALOME

Who is Elias?

SECOND SOLDIER

A prophet of this country in bygone days, Princess.

THE SLAVE

What answer may I give the Tetrarch from the Princess?

THE VOICE OF IOKANAAN

Rejoice not, O land of Palestine, because the rod of him who smote thee is broken. For from the seed of the serpent shall come a basilisk, and that which is born of it shall devour the birds.

SALOME

What a strange voice! I would speak with him.

FIRST SOLDIER

I fear it may not be, Princess. The Tetrarch does not suffer any one to speak with him. He has even forbidden the high priest to speak with him.

SALOME

I desire to speak with him.

FIRST SOLDIER

It is impossible, Princess.

[22]

SALOME
I will speak with him.

THE YOUNG SYRIAN
Would it not be better to return to the banquet?

SALOME
Bring forth this prophet. [*Exit the Slave.*]

FIRST SOLDIER
We dare not, Princess.

SALOME
[*Approaching the cistern and looking down into it.*] How black it is, down there! It must be terrible to be in so black a hole! It is like a tomb. . . . [*To the soldiers.*] Did you not hear me? Bring out the prophet. I would look on him.

SECOND SOLDIER
Princess, I beg you, do not require this of us.

SALOME
You are making me wait upon your pleasure.

FIRST SOLDIER
Princess, our lives belong to you, but we cannot do what you have asked of us. And indeed, it is not of us that you should ask this thing.

SALOME
[*Looking at the young Syrian.*] Ah!

THE PAGE OF HERODIAS
Oh! what is going to happen? I am sure that something terrible will happen.

SALOME
[*Going up to the young Syrian.*] Thou wilt do this thing for me, wilt thou not, Narraboth? Thou wilt do this thing for me. I have ever been kind towards thee. Thou wilt do it for me. I would but look at him, this strange prophet. Men have talked so much of him. Often I have heard the Tetrarch talk of him. I think he is afraid of him, the Tetrarch. Art thou, even thou, also afraid of him, Narraboth?

THE YOUNG SYRIAN
I fear him not, Princess; there is no man I fear. But the Tetrarch has formally forbidden that any man should raise the cover of this well.

SALOME
Thou wilt do this thing for me, Narraboth, and to-morrow when I pass in my litter beneath the gateway of the idol-sellers I will let fall for thee a little flower, a little green flower.

THE YOUNG SYRIAN
Princess, I cannot, I cannot.

SALOME
[*Smiling.*] Thou wilt do this thing for me, Narraboth. Thou

knowest that thou wilt do this thing for me. And on the morrow when I shall pass in my litter by the bridge of the idol-buyers, I will look at thee through the muslin veils. I will look at thee, Narraboth, it may be I will smile at thee. Look at me, Narraboth, look at me. Ah! thou knowest that thou wilt do what I ask of thee. Thou knowest it. . . . I know that thou wilt do this thing.

THE YOUNG SYRIAN

[*Signing to the third Soldier.*] Let the prophet come forth. . . . The Princess Salome desires to see him.

SALOME

Ah!

THE PAGE OF HERODIAS

Oh! How strange the moon looks! Like the hand of a dead woman who is seeking to cover herself with a shroud.

THE YOUNG SYRIAN

She has a strange aspect! She is like a little princess, whose eyes are eyes of amber. Through the clouds of muslin she is smiling like a little princess. [*The prophet comes out of the cistern. Salome looks at him and steps slowly back.*]

IOKANAAN

Where is he whose cup of abominations is now full? Where is he, who in a robe of silver shall one day die in the face of all the people? Bid him come forth, that he may hear the voice of him who hath cried in the waste places and in the houses of kings.

SALOME

Of whom is he speaking?

THE YOUNG SYRIAN

No one can tell, Princess.

IOKANAAN

Where is she who saw the images of men painted on the walls, even the images of the Chaldæans painted with colours, and gave herself up unto the lust of her eyes, and sent ambassadors into the land of Chaldæa?

SALOME

It is of my mother that he is speaking.

THE YOUNG SYRIAN

Oh no, Princess.

SALOME

Yes: it is of my mother that he is speaking.

IOKANAAN

Where is she who gave herself unto the Captains of Assyria, who have baldricks on their loins, and crowns of many colours on their heads? Where is she who hath given herself to the young men of the Egyptians, who are clothed in fine linen and hyacinth, whose shields are of gold, whose helmets are of silver, whose bodies are mighty? Go, bid her rise up from the bed of her abominations, from the bed of her incestuousness, that she may hear the words of him who prepareth the way of the Lord, that she may repent her of her iniquities. Though she will not repent, but will stick fast in her abominations, go bid her come, for the fan of the Lord is in His hand.

SALOME

Ah, but he is terrible, he is terrible!

THE YOUNG SYRIAN

Do not stay here, Princess, I beseech you.

SALOME

It is his eyes above all that are terrible. They are like black holes burned by torches in a tapestry of Tyre. They are like the black caverns where the dragons live, the black caverns of Egypt in which the dragons make their lairs. They are like black lakes troubled by fantastic moons.... Do you think he will speak again?

THE YOUNG SYRIAN

Do not stay here, Princess. I pray you do not stay here.

SALOME

How wasted he is! He is like a thin ivory statue. He is like an image of silver. I am sure he is chaste, as the moon is. He is like a moonbeam, like a shaft of silver. His flesh must be very cold, cold as ivory.... I would look closer at him.

THE YOUNG SYRIAN

No, no, Princess!

SALOME

I must look at him closer.

THE YOUNG SYRIAN

Princess! Princess!

IOKANAAN

Who is this woman who is looking at me? I will not have her look at me. Wherefore doth she look at me, with her golden eyes, under her gilded eyelids? I know not who she is. I do not desire to know who she is. Bid her begone. It is not to her that I would speak.

SALOME

I am Salome, daughter of Herodias, Princess of Judæa.

IOKANAAN

Back! daughter of Babylon! Come not near the chosen of the Lord. Thy mother hath filled the earth with the wine of her iniquities, and the cry of her sinning hath come up even to the ears of God.

SALOME

Speak again, Iokanaan. Thy voice is as music to mine ear.

bodies are nought? Oh! bid her she sup from the loaded tables not. On the bed of her incontinence, that the jews have the souls of him who repented the ways of the Lord, that she come upon her for iniquities. I beseech thee will not repent, but will suck fast in her abominations, go bid her come, for the love of the Lord is in His hand.

Ah, but he is terrible, he is terrible.

THE YOUNG SYRIAN

Do not stay here, Princess, I beseech you.

SALOMÉ

It is his eyes above all that are terrible. They are like black holes burned by torches in a tapestry of Tyre. They are like the black caverns where the dragons live, the black caverns of Egypt in which the dragons make their lairs. They are like black lakes troubled by fantastic moons... Do you think he will speak again?

THE YOUNG SYRIAN

Do not stay here, Princess. I pray you do not stay here.

SALOMÉ

How wasted he is! He is like a thin ivory statue. He is like an image of silver. I am sure he is chaste, as the moon is. He is like a moonbeam, like a shaft of silver. His flesh must be very cold, cold as ivory... I would look closer at him.

THE YOUNG SYRIAN

No, no, Princess.

SALOMÉ

I must look at him closer.

THE YOUNG SYRIAN

Princess! Princess!

SALOMÉ

Who is this woman who is looking at me? I will not have her look at me. Wherefore doth she look at me with her golden eyes, under her gilded eyelids? I know not who she is. I do not want to know who she is. Bid her begone. It is not to her that I would speak.

JOKANAAN

I am Salome, daughter of Herodias, Princess of Judea.

JOKANAAN

Back! daughter of Babylon! Come not near the chosen of the Lord. Thy mother hath filled the earth with the wine of her iniquities, and the cry of her sinning hath come up even to the ears of God.

SALOMÉ

Speak again, Jokanaan. Thy voice is as wine to mine ear.

THE YOUNG SYRIAN

Princess! Princess! Princess!

SALOME

Speak again! Speak again, Iokanaan, and tell me what I must do.

IOKANAAN

Daughter of Sodom, come not near me! But cover thy face with a veil, and scatter ashes upon thine head, and get thee to the desert, and seek out the Son of Man.

SALOME

Who is he, the Son of Man? Is he as beautiful as thou art, Iokanaan?

IOKANAAN

Get thee behind me! I hear in the palace the beating of the wings of the angel of death.

THE YOUNG SYRIAN

Princess, I beseech thee to go within.

IOKANAAN

Angel of the Lord God, what dost thou here with thy sword? Whom seekest thou in this palace? The day of him who shall die in a robe of silver has not yet come.

SALOME

Iokanaan!

IOKANAAN

Who speaketh?

SALOME

I am amorous of thy body, Iokanaan! Thy body is white, like the lilies of a field that the mower hath never mowed. Thy body is white like the snows that lie on the mountains of Judæa, and come down into the valleys. The roses in the garden of the Queen of Arabia are not so white as thy body. Neither the roses of the garden of the Queen of Arabia, the garden of spices of the Queen of Arabia, nor the feet of the dawn when they light on the leaves, nor the breast of the moon when she lies on the breast of the sea. . . . There is nothing in the world so white as thy body. Suffer me to touch thy body.

IOKANAAN

Back! daughter of Babylon! By woman came evil into the world. Speak not to me. I will not listen to thee. I listen but to the voice of the Lord God.

SALOME

Thy body is hideous. It is like the body of a leper. It is like a plastered wall, where vipers have crawled; like a plastered wall where the scorpions have made their nest. It is like a whited sepulchre, full of loathsome things. It is horrible, thy body is horrible. It is of thy hair that I am enamoured, Iokanaan. Thy hair

[26]

is like clusters of grapes, like the clusters of black grapes that hang from the vine-trees of Edom in the land of the Edomites. Thy hair is like the cedars of Lebanon, like the great cedars of Lebanon that give their shade to the lions and to the robbers who would hide them by day. The long black nights, when the moon hides her face, when the stars are afraid, are not so black as thy hair. The silence that dwells in the forest is not so black. There is nothing in the world that is so black as thy hair.... Suffer me to touch thy hair.

IOKANAAN

Back, daughter of Sodom! Touch me not. Profane not the temple of the Lord God.

SALOME

Thy hair is horrible. It is covered with mire and dust. It is like a crown of thorns placed on thy head. It is like a knot of serpents coiled round thy neck. I love not thy hair.... It is thy mouth that I desire, Iokanaan. Thy mouth is like a band of scarlet on a tower of ivory. It is like a pomegranate cut in twain with a knife of ivory. The pomegranate flowers that blossom in the gardens of Tyre, and are redder than roses, are not so red. The red blasts of trumpets that herald the approach of kings, and make afraid the enemy, are not so red. Thy mouth is redder than the feet of those who tread the wine in the wine-press. It is redder than the feet of the doves who inhabit the temples and are fed by the priests. It is redder than the feet of him who cometh from a forest where he hath slain a lion, and seen gilded tigers. Thy mouth is like a branch of coral that fishers have found in the twilight of the sea, the coral that they keep for kings! ... It is like the vermilion that the Moabites find in the mines of Moab, the vermilion that the kings take from them. It is like the bow of the King of the Persians, that is painted with vermilion, and is tipped with coral. There is nothing in the world so red as thy mouth.... Suffer me to kiss thy mouth.

IOKANAAN

Never! daughter of Babylon! Daughter of Sodom! never!

SALOME

I will kiss thy mouth, Iokanaan. I will kiss thy mouth.

THE YOUNG SYRIAN

Princess, Princess, thou who art like a garden of myrrh, thou who art the dove of all doves, look not at this man, look not at him! Do not speak such words to him. I cannot endure it.... Princess, do not speak these things.

SALOME

I will kiss thy mouth, Iokanaan.

[27]

is like clusters of grapes, like the clusters of black grapes that hang from the vine-trees of Edom in the land of the Edomites. Thy hair is like the cedars of Lebanon, like the great cedars of Lebanon that give their shade to the lions and to the robbers who would hide them by day. The long black nights, when the moon hides her face, when the stars are afraid, are not so black as thy hair. The silence that dwells in the forest is not so black. There is nothing in the world that is so black as thy hair.... Suffer me to touch thy hair.

IOKANAAN

Back, daughter of Sodom! Touch me not. Profane not the temple of the Lord God.

SALOMÉ

Thy hair is horrible. It is covered with mire and dust. It is like a crown of thorns placed on thy head. It is like a knot of serpents coiled round thy neck. I love not thy hair.... It is thy mouth that I desire, Iokanaan. Thy mouth is like a band of scarlet on a tower of ivory. It is like a pomegranate cut in twain with a knife of ivory. The pomegranate flowers that blossom in the gardens of Tyre, and are redder than roses, are not so red. The red blasts of trumpets that herald the approach of kings, and make afraid the enemy, are not so red. Thy mouth is redder than the feet of those who tread the wine in the wine-press. It is redder than the feet of the doves who inhabit the temples and are fed by the priests. It is redder than the feet of him who cometh from a forest where he hath slain a lion, and seen gilded tigers. Thy mouth is like a branch of coral that fishers have found in the twilight of the sea, the coral that they keep for kings!... It is like the vermilion that the Moabites find in the mines of Moab, the vermilion that the kings take from them. It is like the bow of the King of the Persians, that is painted with vermilion, and is tipped with coral. There is nothing in the world so red as thy mouth.... Suffer me to kiss thy mouth.

IOKANAAN

Never! daughter of Babylon! Daughter of Sodom! never!

SALOMÉ

I will kiss thy mouth, Iokanaan; I will kiss thy mouth.

THE YOUNG SYRIAN

Princess, Princess, thou who art like a garden of myrrh, thou who art the dove of all doves, look not at this man, look not at him! To not speak such words to him. I cannot endure it.... Princess, do not speak these things.

SALOMÉ

I will kiss thy mouth, Iokanaan.

[54]

Ah! (*He dies, and falls between Salomé and Jokanaan.*)

THE PAGE OF HERODIAS.

The young Syrian has slain himself! The young captain has slain himself! He has slain himself who was my friend! I gave him a little box of perfumes and ear-rings wrought in silver, and now he has killed himself! Ah, did he not say that some misfortune would happen. I, too, said it, and it has come to pass. Well I knew that the moon was seeking a dead thing, but I knew not that it was he whom she sought. Ah! why did I not hide him from the moon? If I had hidden him in a cavern she would not have seen him.

FIRST SOLDIER.

Princess, the young captain has just slain himself.

SALOMÉ.

Suffer me to kiss thy mouth, Jokanaan.

JOKANAAN.

Art thou not afraid, daughter of Herodias? Did I not tell thee that I had heard in the palace the beating of the wings of the angel of death, and hath he not come, the angel of death?

SALOMÉ.

Suffer me to kiss thy mouth.

JOKANAAN.

Daughter of adultery, there is but one who can save thee. It is He of whom I spake. Go seek Him. He is in a boat on the sea of Galilee, and He talketh with His disciples. Kneel down on the shore of the sea, and call unto Him by His name. When He cometh to thee, and to all who call on Him He cometh, bow thyself at His feet and ask of Him the remission of thy sins.

SALOMÉ.

Suffer me to kiss thy mouth.

JOKANAAN.

Cursed be thou! daughter of an incestuous mother, be thou accursed!

SALOMÉ.

I will kiss thy mouth, Jokanaan.

JOKANAAN.

I will not look at thee. Thou art accursed, Salomé, thou art accursed. (*He goes down into the cistern.*)

SALOMÉ.

I will kiss thy mouth, Jokanaan, I will kiss thy mouth.

FIRST SOLDIER.

We must bear away the body to another place. The Tetrarch does not care to see dead bodies, save the bodies of those whom he himself has slain.

THE YOUNG SYRIAN

Ah! [*He kills himself, and falls between Salome and Iokanaan.*]

THE PAGE OF HERODIAS

The young Syrian has slain himself! The young captain has slain himself! He has slain himself who was my friend! I gave him a little box of perfumes and ear-rings wrought in silver, and now he has killed himself! Ah, did he not say that some misfortune would happen? I, too, said it, and it has come to pass. Well I knew that the moon was seeking a dead thing, but I knew not that it was he whom she sought. Ah! why did I not hide him from the moon? If I had hidden him in a cavern she would not have seen him.

FIRST SOLDIER

Princess, the young captain has just slain himself.

SALOME

Suffer me to kiss thy mouth, Iokanaan.

IOKANAAN

Art thou not afraid, daughter of Herodias? Did I not tell thee that I had heard in the palace the beating of the wings of the angel of death, and hath he not come, the angel of death?

SALOME

Suffer me to kiss thy mouth.

IOKANAAN

Daughter of adultery, there is but one who can save thee. It is He of whom I spake. Go seek Him. He is in a boat on the sea of Galilee, and He talketh with His disciples. Kneel down on the shore of the sea, and call unto Him by His name. When He cometh to thee, and to all who call on Him He cometh, bow thyself at His feet and ask of Him the remission of thy sins.

SALOME

Suffer me to kiss thy mouth.

IOKANAAN

Cursed be thou! daughter of an incestuous mother, be thou accursed!

SALOME

I will kiss thy mouth, Iokanaan.

IOKANAAN

I will not look at thee. Thou art accursed, Salome, thou art accursed. [*He goes down into the cistern.*]

SALOME

I will kiss thy mouth, Iokanaan; I will kiss thy mouth.

FIRST SOLDIER

We must bear away the body to another place. The Tetrarch does not care to see dead bodies, save the bodies of those whom he himself has slain.

[28]

He was my brother, and nearer to me than a brother. I gave him a little box full of perfumes, and a ring of agate that he always wore on his hand. In the evening we were wont to walk by the river, and among the almond-trees, and he used to tell me of the things of his country. He spake ever very low. The sound of his voice was like the sound of the flute, of one who playeth upon the flute. Also he had much joy to gaze at himself in the river. I used to reproach him for that.

SECOND SOLDIER

You are right; we must hide the body. The Tetrarch must not see it.

FIRST SOLDIER

The Tetrarch will not come to this place. He never comes on the terrace. He is too much afraid of the prophet.

[Enter Herod, Herodias, and all the Court.]

HEROD

Where is Salomé? Where is the Princess? Why did she not return to the banquet as I commanded her? Ah! there she is!

HERODIAS

You must not look at her! You are always looking at her!

HEROD

The moon has a strange look to-night. Has she not a strange look? She is like a mad woman, a mad woman who is seeking everywhere for lovers. She is naked too. She is quite naked. The clouds are seeking to clothe her nakedness, but she will not let them. She shows herself naked in the sky. She reels through the clouds like a drunken woman. . . . I am sure she is looking for lovers. Does she not reel like a drunken woman? She is like a mad woman, is she not?

HERODIAS

No; the moon is like the moon, that is all. Let us go within. . . . We have nothing to do here.

HEROD

I will stay here, Manasseh! Lay carpets there. Light torches. Bring forth the ivory tables, and the tables of jasper. The air here is sweet. I will drink more wine with my guests. We must show all honours to the ambassadors of Caesar.

HERODIAS

It is not because of them that you remain.

HEROD

Yes; the air is very sweet. Come, Herodias, our guests await us. Ah! I have slipped! I have slipped in blood! It is an ill omen. It is a very ill omen. Wherefore is there blood here? . . . and this body, what does this body here? Think you I am like the King

THE PAGE OF HERODIAS

He was my brother, and nearer to me than a brother. I gave him a little box full of perfumes, and a ring of agate that he wore always on his hand. In the evening we were wont to walk by the river, and among the almond-trees, and he used to tell me of the things of his country. He spake ever very low. The sound of his voice was like the sound of the flute, of one who playeth upon the flute. Also he had much joy to gaze at himself in the river. I used to reproach him for that.

SECOND SOLDIER

You are right; we must hide the body. The Tetrarch must not see it.

FIRST SOLDIER

The Tetrarch will not come to this place. He never comes on the terrace. He is too much afraid of the prophet.

[*Enter Herod, Herodias, and all the Court.*]

HEROD

Where is Salome? Where is the Princess? Why did she not return to the banquet as I commanded her? Ah! there she is!

HERODIAS

You must not look at her! You are always looking at her!

HEROD

The moon has a strange look to-night. Has she not a strange look? She is like a mad woman, a mad woman who is seeking everywhere for lovers. She is naked too. She is quite naked. The clouds are seeking to clothe her nakedness, but she will not let them. She shows herself naked in the sky. She reels through the clouds like a drunken woman.... I am sure she is looking for lovers. Does she not reel like a drunken woman? She is like a mad woman, is she not?

HERODIAS

No; the moon is like the moon, that is all. Let us go within.... We have nothing to do here.

HEROD

I will stay here! Manasseh, lay carpets there. Light torches. Bring forth the ivory tables, and the tables of jasper. The air here is sweet. I will drink more wine with my guests. We must show all honours to the ambassadors of Cæsar.

HERODIAS

It is not because of them that you remain.

HEROD

Yes; the air is very sweet. Come, Herodias, our guests await us. Ah! I have slipped! I have slipped in blood! It is an ill omen. It is a very ill omen. Wherefore is there blood here?... and this body, what does this body here? Think you I am like the King

[30]

of Egypt, who gives no feast to his guests but that he shows them a corpse? Whose is it? I will not look on it.

FIRST SOLDIER

It is our captain, sire. It is the young Syrian whom you made captain of the guard but three days gone.

HEROD

I issued no order that he should be slain.

SECOND SOLDIER

He slew himself, sire.

HEROD

For what reason? I had made him captain of my guard!

SECOND SOLDIER

We do not know, sire. But with his own hand he slew himself.

HEROD

That seems strange to me. I had thought it was but the Roman philosophers who slew themselves. Is it not true, Tigellinus, that the philosophers at Rome slay themselves?

TIGELLINUS

There be some who slay themselves, sire. They are the Stoics. The Stoics are people of no cultivation. They are ridiculous people. I myself regard them as being perfectly ridiculous.

HEROD

I also. It is ridiculous to kill one's-self.

TIGELLINUS

Everybody at Rome laughs at them. The Emperor has written a satire against them. It is recited everywhere.

HEROD

Ah! he has written a satire against them? Cæsar is wonderful. He can do everything. . . . It is strange that the young Syrian has slain himself. I am sorry he has slain himself. I am very sorry. For he was fair to look upon. He was even very fair. He had very languorous eyes. I remember that I saw that he looked languorously at Salome. Truly, I thought he looked too much at her.

HERODIAS

There are others who look too much at her.

HEROD

His father was a king. I drove him from his kingdom. And of his mother, who was a queen, you made a slave, Herodias. So he was here as my guest, as it were, and for that reason I made him my captain. I am sorry he is dead. Ho! why have you left the body here? It must be taken to some other place. I will not look at it,— away with it! [They take away the body.] It is cold here. There is a wind blowing. Is there not a wind blowing?

[31]

HERODIAS

No; there is no wind.

HEROD

I tell you there is a wind that blows. . . . And I hear in the air something that is like the beating of wings, like the beating of vast wings. Do you not hear it?

HERODIAS

I hear nothing.

HEROD

I hear it no longer. But I heard it. It was the blowing of the wind. It has passed away. But no, I hear it again. Do you not hear it? It is just like a beating of wings.

HERODIAS

I tell you there is nothing. You are ill. Let us go within.

HEROD

I am not ill. It is your daughter who is sick to death. Never have I seen her so pale.

HERODIAS

I have told you not to look at her.

HEROD

Pour me forth wine. [*Wine is brought.*] Salome, come drink a little wine with me. I have here a wine that is exquisite. Cæsar himself sent it me. Dip into it thy little red lips, that I may drain the cup.

SALOME

I am not thirsty, Tetrarch.

HEROD

You hear how she answers me, this daughter of yours?

HERODIAS

She does right. Why are you always gazing at her?

HEROD

Bring me ripe fruits. [*Fruits are brought.*] Salome, come and eat fruits with me. I love to see in a fruit the mark of thy little teeth. Bite but a little of this fruit, that I may eat what is left.

SALOME

I am not hungry, Tetrarch.

HEROD

[*To Herodias.*] You see how you have brought up this daughter of yours.

HERODIAS

My daughter and I come of a royal race. As for thee, thy father was a camel driver! He was a thief and a robber to boot!

HEROD

Thou liest!

HERODIAS

Thou knowest well that it is true.

[32]

HEROD

Salome, come and sit next to me. I will give thee the throne of thy mother.

SALOME

I am not tired, Tetrarch.

HERODIAS

You see in what regard she holds you.

HEROD

Bring me—What is it that I desire? I forget. Ah! ah! I remember.

THE VOICE OF IOKANAAN

Behold the time is come! That which I foretold has come to pass. The day that I spake of is at hand.

HERODIAS

Bid him be silent. I will not listen to his voice. This man is for ever hurling insults against me.

HEROD

He has said nothing against you. Besides, he is a very great prophet.

HERODIAS

I do not believe in prophets. Can a man tell what will come to pass? No man knows it. Also he is for ever insulting me. But I think you are afraid of him. . . . I know well that you are afraid of him.

HEROD

I am not afraid of him. I am afraid of no man.

HERODIAS

I tell you you are afraid of him. If you are not afraid of him why do you not deliver him to the Jews who for these six months past have been clamouring for him?

A JEW

Truly, my lord, it were better to deliver him into our hands.

HEROD

Enough on this subject. I have already given you my answer. I will not deliver him into your hands. He is a holy man. He is a man who has seen God.

A JEW

That cannot be. There is no man who hath seen God since the prophet Elias. He is the last man who saw God face to face. In these days God doth not show Himself. God hideth Himself. Therefore great evils have come upon the land.

ANOTHER JEW

Verily, no man knoweth if Elias the prophet did indeed see God. Peradventure it was but the shadow of God that he saw.

A THIRD JEW

God is at no time hidden. He showeth Himself at all times

and in all places. God is in what is evil even as He is in what is good.

A FOURTH JEW

Thou shouldst not say that. It is a very dangerous doctrine. It is a doctrine that cometh from Alexandria, where men teach the philosophy of the Greeks. And the Greeks are Gentiles. They are not even circumcised.

A FIFTH JEW

No man can tell how God worketh. His ways are very dark. It may be that the things which we call evil are good, and that the things which we call good are evil. There is no knowledge of anything. We cannot but bow our heads to His will, for God is very strong. He breaketh in pieces the strong together with the weak, for He regardeth not any man.

FIRST JEW

Thou speakest truly. Verily, God is terrible. He breaketh in pieces the strong and the weak as men break corn in a mortar. But as for this man, he hath never seen God. No man hath seen God since the prophet Elias.

HERODIAS

Make them be silent. They weary me.

HEROD

But I have heard it said that Iokanaan is in very truth your prophet Elias.

THE JEW

That cannot be. It is more than three hundred years since the days of the prophet Elias.

HEROD

There be some who say that this man is Elias the prophet.

A NAZARENE

I am sure that he is Elias the prophet.

THE JEW

Nay, but he is not Elias the prophet.

THE VOICE OF IOKANAAN

Behold the day is at hand, the day of the Lord, and I hear upon the mountains the feet of Him who shall be the Saviour of the world.

HEROD

What does that mean? The Saviour of the world?

TIGELLINUS

It is a title that Cæsar adopts.

HEROD

But Cæsar is not coming into Judæa. Only yesterday I received letters from Rome. They contained nothing concerning this matter. And you, Tigellinus, who were at Rome during the winter, you heard nothing concerning this matter, did you?

TIGELLINUS

Sire, I heard nothing concerning the matter. I was but explaining the title. It is one of Cæsar's titles.

HEROD

But Cæsar cannot come. He is too gouty. They say that his feet are like the feet of an elephant. Also there are reasons of state. He who leaves Rome loses Rome. He will not come. Howbeit, Cæsar is lord, he will come if such be his pleasure. Nevertheless, I think he will not come.

FIRST NAZARENE

It was not concerning Cæsar that the prophet spake these words, sire.

HEROD

How?—it was not concerning Cæsar?

FIRST NAZARENE

No, my lord.

HEROD

Concerning whom then did he speak?

FIRST NAZARENE

Concerning Messias, who hath come.

A JEW

Messias hath not come.

FIRST NAZARENE

He hath come, and everywhere He worketh miracles!

HERODIAS

Ho! ho! miracles! I do not believe in miracles. I have seen too many. [*To the Page.*] My fan.

FIRST NAZARENE

This Man worketh true miracles. Thus, at a marriage which took place in a little town of Galilee, a town of some importance, He changed water into wine. Certain persons who were present related it to me. Also He healed two lepers that were seated before the Gate of Capernaum simply by touching them.

SECOND NAZARENE

Nay; it was two blind men that He healed at Capernaum.

FIRST NAZARENE

Nay; they were lepers. But He hath healed blind people also, and He was seen on a mountain talking with angels.

A SADDUCEE

Angels do not exist.

A PHARISEE

Angels exist but I do not believe that this Man has talked with them.

FIRST NAZARENE

He was seen by a great multitude of people talking with angels.

[35]

HERODIAS

How these men weary me! They are ridiculous! They are altogether ridiculous! [*To the Page.*] Well! my fan? [*The Page gives her the fan.*] You have a dreamer's look. You must not dream. It is only sick people who dream. [*She strikes the Page with her fan.*]

SECOND NAZARENE

There is also the miracle of the daughter of Jairus.

FIRST NAZARENE

Yea, that is sure. No man can gainsay it.

HERODIAS

Those men are mad. They have looked too long on the moon. Command them to be silent.

HEROD

What is this miracle of the daughter of Jairus?

FIRST NAZARENE

The daughter of Jairus was dead. This Man raised her from the dead.

HEROD

How! He raises people from the dead?

FIRST NAZARENE

Yea, sire; He raiseth the dead.

HEROD

I do not wish Him to do that. I forbid Him to do that. I suffer no man to raise the dead. This Man must be found and told that I forbid Him to raise the dead. Where is this Man at present?

SECOND NAZARENE

He is in every place, my lord, but it is hard to find Him.

FIRST NAZARENE

It is said that He is now in Samaria.

A JEW

It is easy to see that this is not Messias, if He is in Samaria. It is not to the Samaritans that Messias shall come. The Samaritans are accursed. They bring no offerings to the Temple.

SECOND NAZARENE

He left Samaria a few days since. I think that at the present moment He is in the neighbourhood of Jerusalem.

FIRST NAZARENE

No; He is not there. I have just come from Jerusalem. For two months they have had no tidings of Him.

HEROD

No matter! But let them find Him, and tell Him, thus saith Herod the King, 'I will not suffer Thee to raise the dead.' To change water into wine, to heal the lepers and the blind. . . . He may do these things if He will. I say nothing against these things. In truth I hold it a kindly deed to heal a leper. But no man shall

raise the dead.... It would be terrible if the dead came back.

THE VOICE OF IOKANAAN

Ah! The wanton one! The harlot! Ah! the daughter of Babylon with her golden eyes and her gilded eyelids! Thus saith the Lord God. Let there come up against her a multitude of men. Let the people take stones and stone her....

HERODIAS

Command him to be silent.

THE VOICE OF IOKANAAN

Let the captains of the hosts pierce her with their swords, let them crush her beneath their shields.

HERODIAS

Nay, but it is infamous.

THE VOICE OF IOKANAAN

It is thus that I will wipe out all wickedness from the earth, and that all women shall learn not to imitate her abominations.

HERODIAS

You hear what he says against me? You suffer him to revile her who is your wife?

HEROD

He did not speak your name.

HERODIAS

What does that matter? You know well that it is I whom he seeks to revile. And I am your wife, am I not?

HEROD

Of a truth, dear and noble Herodias, you are my wife, and before that you were the wife of my brother.

HERODIAS

It was thou didst snatch me from his arms.

HEROD

Of a truth I was stronger than he was.... But let us not talk of that matter. I do not desire to talk of it. It is the cause of the terrible words that the prophet has spoken. Peradventure on account of it a misfortune will come. Let us not speak of this matter. Noble Herodias, we are not mindful of our guests. Fill thou my cup, my well-beloved. Ho! fill with wine the great goblets of silver, and the great goblets of glass. I will drink to Cæsar. There are Romans here, we must drink to Cæsar.

[Vin. Cæsar! Cæsar!]

HEROD

Do you not see your daughter, how pale she is?

HERODIAS

What is it to you if she be pale or not?

HEROD

Never have I seen her so pale.

raise the dead. . . . It would be terrible if the dead came back.

THE VOICE OF IOKANAAN

Ah! The wanton one! The harlot! Ah! the daughter of Babylon with her golden eyes and her gilded eyelids! Thus saith the Lord God, Let there come up against her a multitude of men. Let the people take stones and stone her. . . .

HERODIAS

Command him to be silent!

THE VOICE OF IOKANAAN

Let the captains of the hosts pierce her with their swords, let them crush her beneath their shields.

HERODIAS

Nay, but it is infamous.

THE VOICE OF IOKANAAN

It is thus that I will wipe out all wickedness from the earth, and that all women shall learn not to imitate her abominations.

HERODIAS

You hear what he says against me? You suffer him to revile her who is your wife!

HEROD

He did not speak your name.

HERODIAS

What does that matter? You know well that it is I whom he seeks to revile. And I am your wife, am I not?

HEROD

Of a truth, dear and noble Herodias, you are my wife, and before that you were the wife of my brother.

HERODIAS

It was thou didst snatch me from his arms.

HEROD

Of a truth I was stronger than he was. . . . But let us not talk of that matter. I do not desire to talk of it. It is the cause of the terrible words that the prophet has spoken. Peradventure on account of it a misfortune will come. Let us not speak of this matter. Noble Herodias, we are not mindful of our guests. Fill thou my cup, my well-beloved. Ho! fill with wine the great goblets of silver, and the great goblets of glass. I will drink to Cæsar. There are Romans here, we must drink to Cæsar.

[ALL: Cæsar! Cæsar!]

HEROD

Do you not see your daughter, how pale she is?

HERODIAS

What is it to you if she be pale or not?

HEROD

Never have I seen her so pale.

HERODIAS

You must not look at her.

THE VOICE OF IOKANAAN

In that day the sun shall become black like sackcloth of hair, and the moon shall become like blood, and the stars of the heaven shall fall upon the earth like unripe figs that fall from the fig-tree, and the kings of the earth shall be afraid.

HERODIAS

Ah! ah! I should like to see that day of which he speaks, when the moon shall become like blood, and when the stars shall fall upon the earth like unripe figs. This prophet talks like a drunken man . . . but I cannot suffer the sound of his voice. I hate his voice. Command him to be silent.

HEROD

I will not. I cannot understand what it is that he saith, but it may be an omen.

HERODIAS

I do not believe in omens. He speaks like a drunken man.

HEROD

It may be he is drunk with the wine of God.

HERODIAS

What wine is that, the wine of God? From what vineyards is it gathered? In what wine-press may one find it?

HEROD

[*From this point he looks all the while at Salome.*] Tigellinus, when you were at Rome of late, did the Emperor speak with you on the subject of . . .?

TIGELLINUS

On what subject, my lord?

HEROD

On what subject? Ah! I asked you a question, did I not? I have forgotten what I would have asked you.

HERODIAS

You are looking again at my daughter. You must not look at her. I have already said so.

HEROD

You say nothing else.

HERODIAS

I say it again.

HEROD

And that restoration of the Temple about which they have talked so much, will anything be done? They say that the veil of the Sanctuary has disappeared, do they not?

HERODIAS

It was thyself didst steal it. Thou speakest at random and without wit. I will not stay here. Let us go within.

[39]

HEROD

Dance for me, Salome.

HERODIAS

I will not have her dance.

SALOME

I have no desire to dance, Tetrarch.

HEROD

Salome, daughter of Herodias, dance for me.

HERODIAS

Peace. Let her alone.

HEROD

I command thee to dance, Salome.

SALOME

I will not dance, Tetrarch.

HERODIAS

[*Laughing.*] You see how she obeys you.

HEROD

What is it to me whether she dance or not? It is nought to me. To-night I am happy. I am exceeding happy. Never have I been so happy.

FIRST SOLDIER

The Tetrarch has a sombre look. Has he not a sombre look?

SECOND SOLDIER

Yes, he has a sombre look.

HEROD

Wherefore should I not be happy? Cæsar, who is lord of the world, Cæsar, who is lord of all things, loves me well. He has just sent me most precious gifts. Also he has promised me to summon to Rome the King of Cappadocia, who is mine enemy. It may be that at Rome he will crucify him, for he is able to do all things that he has a mind to do. Verily, Cæsar is lord. Therefore I do well to be happy. I am very happy, never have I been so happy. There is nothing in the world that can mar my happiness.

THE VOICE OF IOKANAAN

He shall be seated on his throne. He shall be clothed in scarlet and purple. In his hand he shall bear a golden cup full of his blasphemies. And the angel of the Lord shall smite him. He shall be eaten of worms.

HERODIAS

You hear what he says about you. He says that you shall be eaten of worms.

HEROD

It is not of me that he speaks. He speaks never against me. It is of the King of Cappadocia that he speaks; the King of Cappadocia who is mine enemy. It is he who shall be eaten of worms.

It is not I. Never has he spoken word against me, this prophet, save that I sinned in taking to wife the wife of my brother. It may be he is right. For, of a truth, you are sterile.

HERODIAS

I am sterile, I? You say that, you that are ever looking at my daughter, you that would have her dance for your pleasure? You speak as a fool. I have borne a child. You have gotten no child, no, not on one of your slaves. It is you who are sterile, not I.

HEROD

Peace, woman! I say that you are sterile. You have borne me no child, and the prophet says that our marriage is not a true marriage. He says that it is a marriage of incest, a marriage that will bring evils. . . . I fear he is right; I am sure that he is right. But it is not the hour to speak of these things. I would be happy at this moment. Of a truth, I am happy. There is nothing I lack.

HERODIAS

I am glad you are of so fair a humour to-night. It is not your custom. But it is late. Let us go within. Do not forget that we hunt at sunrise. All honours must be shown to Cæsar's ambassadors, must they not?

SECOND SOLDIER

The Tetrarch has a sombre look.

FIRST SOLDIER

Yes, he has a sombre look.

HEROD

Salome, Salome, dance for me. I pray thee dance for me. I am sad to-night. Yes, I am passing sad to-night. When I came hither I slipped in blood, which is an ill omen; also I heard in the air a beating of wings, a beating of giant wings. I cannot tell what that may mean. . . . I am sad to-night. Therefore dance for me. Dance for me, Salome, I beseech thee. If thou dancest for me thou mayest ask of me what thou wilt, and I will give it thee. Yes, dance for me, Salome, and whatsoever thou shalt ask of me I will give it thee, even unto the half of my kingdom.

SALOME

[Rising.] Will you indeed give me whatsoever I shall ask of you, Tetrarch?

HERODIAS

Do not dance, my daughter.

HEROD

Whatsoever thou shalt ask of me, even unto the half of my kingdom.

SALOME

You swear it, Tetrarch?

HEROD

I swear it, Salome.

[41]

It is not I. Never has he spoken word against me, this prophet, save that I sinned in taking to wife the wife of my brother. It may be he is right, for, of a truth, you are sterile.

HERODIAS

I am sterile, I? You say that, you that are ever looking at my daughter, you that would have her dance for your pleasure? You speak as a fool. I have borne a child. You have gotten no child, no, not on one of your slaves. It is you who are sterile, not I.

HEROD

Peace, woman! I say that you are sterile. You have borne me no child, and the prophet says that our marriage is not a true marriage. He says that it is a marriage of incest, a marriage that will bring evils.... I fear he is right; I am sure that he is right. But it is not the hour to speak of these things. I would be happy at this moment. Of a truth, I am happy. There is nothing I lack.

HERODIAS

I am glad you are of so fair a humour to-night. It is not your custom. But it is late. Let us go within. Do not forget that we hunt at sunrise. All honours must be shown to Cæsar's ambassadors, must they not?

SECOND SOLDIER

The Tetrarch has a sombre look.

FIRST SOLDIER

Yes, he has a sombre look.

HEROD

Salome, Salome, dance for me. I pray thee dance for me. I am sad to-night. Yes, I am passing sad to-night. When I came hither I slipped in blood, which is an ill omen; also I heard in the air a beating of wings, a beating of giant wings. I cannot tell what that may mean.... I am sad to-night. Therefore dance for me. Dance for me, Salome, I beseech thee. If thou dancest for me thou mayest ask of me what thou wilt, and I will give it thee. Yes, dance for me, Salome, and whatsoever thou shalt ask of me I will give it thee, even unto the half of my kingdom.

SALOME

Will you indeed give me whatsoever I shall ask of you?

HERODIAS

Do not dance, my daughter.

HEROD

Whatsoever thou shalt ask of me, even unto the half of my kingdom.

SALOME

You swear it, Tetrarch?

HEROD

I swear it, Salome.

[81]

HEROD

Dance for me, my daughter.

HERODIAS

. . . . .

By what will you swear this thing, Jehova?

HEROD

By my life, by my crown, by my gods. Whatsoever thou shalt desire I will give it thee, even to the half of my kingdom, if thou wilt but dance for me. O Salomé, Salomé, dance for me!

SALOME

You have sworn an oath, Tetrarch.

HEROD

I have sworn an oath.

HERODIAS

My daughter, do not dance.

HEROD

Even to the half of my kingdom. Thou wilt be passing fair as a queen, Salomé, if it please thee to ask for the half of my kingdom. Will she not be fair as a queen? Ah! it is cold here! There is an icy wind, and I hear . . . wherefore do I hear in the air this beating of wings? Ah! one might fancy a huge black bird that hovers over the terrace. Why can I not see it, this bird? The beat of its wings is terrible. The breath of the wind of its wings is terrible. It is a chill wind. Nay, but it is not cold, it is hot. I am choking. Pour water on my hands. Give me snow to eat. Loosen my mantle. Quick! quick! loosen my mantle. Nay, but leave it. It is my garland that hurts me, my garland of roses. The flowers are like fire. They have burned my forehead. (He tears the wreath from his head, and throws it on the table.) Ah! I can breathe now. How red those petals are! They are like stains of blood on the cloth. That does not matter. It is not wise to find symbols in everything that one sees. It makes life too full of terrors. It were better to say that stains of blood are as lovely as rose petals. It were better far to say that . . . But we will not speak of this. Now I am happy. I am passing happy. Have I not the right to be happy? Your daughter is going to dance for me. Wilt thou not dance for me, Salomé? Thou hast promised to dance for me.

HERODIAS

I will not have her dance.

SALOME

I will dance for you, Tetrarch.

HEROD

You hear what your daughter says. She is going to dance for me. Thou dost well to dance for me, Salomé. And when thou hast danced for me, forget not to ask of me whatsoever thou hast a mind to ask. Whatsoever thou shalt desire I will give it

[83]

HERODIAS

Do not dance, my daughter.

SALOME

By what will you swear this thing, Tetrarch?

HEROD

By my life, by my crown, by my gods. Whatsoever thou shalt
desire I will give it thee, even to the half of my kingdom, if thou
wilt but dance for me. O Salome, Salome, dance for me!

SALOME

You have sworn an oath, Tetrarch.

HEROD

I have sworn an oath.

HERODIAS

My daughter, do not dance.

HEROD

Even to the half of my kingdom. Thou wilt be passing fair as
a queen, Salome, if it please thee to ask for the half of my kingdom. Will she not be fair as a queen? Ah! it is cold here! There
is an icy wind, and I hear ... wherefore do I hear in the air this
beating of wings? Ah! one might fancy a huge black bird that
hovers over the terrace. Why can I not see it, this bird? The beat
of its wings is terrible. The breath of the wind of its wings is
terrible. It is a chill wind. Nay, but it is not cold, it is hot. I am
choking. Pour water on my hands. Give me snow to eat. Loosen
my mantle. Quick! quick! loosen my mantle. Nay, but leave it.
It is my garland that hurts me, my garland of roses. The flowers
are like fire. They have burned my forehead. [*He tears the wreath
from his head, and throws it on the table.*] Ah! I can breathe now.
How red those petals are! They are like stains of blood on the
cloth. That does not matter. It is not wise to find symbols in
everything that one sees. It makes life too full of terrors. It were
better to say that stains of blood are as lovely as rose-petals. It
were better far to say that. . . . But we will not speak of this. Now
I am happy. I am passing happy. Have I not the right to be
happy? Your daughter is going to dance for me. Wilt thou not
dance for me, Salome? Thou hast promised to dance for me.

HERODIAS

I will not have her dance.

SALOME

I will dance for you, Tetrarch.

HEROD

You hear what your daughter says. She is going to dance for
me. Thou doest well to dance for me, Salome. And when thou
hast danced for me, forget not to ask of me whatsoever thou
hast a mind to ask. Whatsoever thou shalt desire I will give it

thee, even to the half of my kingdom. I have sworn it, have I not?

SALOME

Thou hast sworn it, Tetrarch.

HEROD

And I have never failed of my word. I am not of those who break their oaths. I know not how to lie. I am the slave of my word, and my word is the word of a king. The King of Cappadocia had ever a lying tongue, but he is no true king. He is a coward. Also he owes me money that he will not repay. He has even insulted my ambassadors. He has spoken words that were wounding. But Cæsar will crucify him when he comes to Rome. I know that Cæsar will crucify him. And if he crucify him not, yet will he die, being eaten of worms. The prophet has prophesied it. Well! Wherefore dost thou tarry, Salome?

SALOME

I am waiting until my slaves bring perfumes to me and the seven veils, and take from off my feet my sandals. [*Slaves bring perfumes and the seven veils, and take off the sandals of Salome.*]

HEROD

Ah, thou art to dance with naked feet! 'Tis well! 'Tis well! Thy little feet will be like white doves. They will be like little white flowers that dance upon the trees. . . . No, no, she is going to dance on blood! There is blood spilt on the ground. She must not dance on blood. It were an evil omen.

HERODIAS

What is it to thee if she dance on blood? Thou hast waded deep enough in it. . . .

HEROD

What is it to me? Ah! look at the moon! She has become red. She has become red as blood. Ah! the prophet prophesied truly. He prophesied that the moon would become as blood. Did he not prophesy it? All of ye heard him prophesying it. And now the moon has become as blood. Do ye not see it?

HERODIAS

Oh yes, I see it well, and the stars are falling like unripe figs, are they not? and the sun is becoming black like sackcloth of hair, and the kings of the earth are afraid. That at least one can see. The prophet is justified of his words in that at least, for truly the kings of the earth are afraid. . . . Let us go within. You are sick. They will say at Rome that you are mad. Let us go within, I tell you.

THE VOICE OF IOKANAAN

Who is this who cometh from Edom, who is this who cometh from Bozra, whose raiment is dyed with purple, who shineth in

the voice of that man maddens me. I will not
have my daughter dance while he is incessantly crying out. I will
not have her dance while you look at her in this fashion. In a
word, I will not have her dance.

THE TETRARCH. ...not that, my queen, it will avail thee nothing. I
will not go within till she hath danced. Dance, Salome, dance
for me.

HERODIAS. I will not have her dance.

SALOME. I am ready, Tetrarch.

[Salome dances the dance of the seven veils.]

HEROD. Ah! wonderful! wonderful! You see that she has danced for me,
your daughter. Come near, Salome, come near, that I may give
thee thy fee. Ah! I pay a royal price to those who dance for my
pleasure. I will pay thee royally. I will give thee whatsoever thy
soul desireth. What wouldst thou have? Speak.

SALOME. I would that they presently bring me in a silver
charger...

HEROD. In a silver charger? Surely yes, in a silver charger. She
is charming, is she not? What is it that thou wouldst have in a
silver charger, O sweet and fair Salome, thou that art fairer than
all the daughters of Judæa? What wouldst thou have them bring
thee in a silver charger? Tell me. Whatsoever it may be, thou
shalt receive it. My treasures belong to thee. What is it that thou
wouldst have, Salome?

SALOME. The head of Jokanaan.

HERODIAS. Ah! that is well said, my daughter.

HEROD. No, no.

HERODIAS. That is well said, my daughter.

HEROD. No, no, Salome. It is not that thou desirest. Do not listen to thy
mother's voice. She gives thee ever evil counsel. Do not heed her.

SALOME. It is not my mother's voice that I heed. It is for mine own pleasure the beauty of his garments, who walketh mighty in his greatness? Wherefore is thy raiment stained with scarlet?

HERODIAS

Let us go within. The voice of that man maddens me. I will not have my daughter dance while he is continually crying out. I will not have her dance while you look at her in this fashion. In a word, I will not have her dance.

HEROD

Do not rise, my wife, my queen, it will avail thee nothing. I will not go within till she hath danced. Dance, Salome, dance for me.

HERODIAS

Do not dance, my daughter.

SALOME

I am ready, Tetrarch.

[Salome dances the dance of the seven veils.]

HEROD

Ah! wonderful! wonderful! You see that she has danced for me, your daughter. Come near, Salome, come near, that I may give thee thy fee. Ah! I pay a royal price to those who dance for my pleasure. I will pay thee royally. I will give thee whatsoever thy soul desireth. What wouldst thou have? Speak.

SALOME

[Kneeling.] I would that they presently bring me in a silver charger ...

HEROD

[Laughing.] In a silver charger? Surely yes, in a silver charger. She is charming, is she not? What is it that thou wouldst have in a silver charger, O sweet and fair Salome, thou that art fairer than all the daughters of Judæa? What wouldst thou have them bring thee in a silver charger? Tell me. Whatsoever it may be, thou shalt receive it. My treasures belong to thee. What is it that thou wouldst have, Salome?

SALOME

[Rising.] The head of Iokanaan.

HERODIAS

Ah! that is well said, my daughter.

HEROD

No, no!

HERODIAS

That is well said, my daughter.

HEROD

No, no, Salome. It is not that thou desirest. Do not listen to thy mother's voice. She gives thee evil counsel. Do not heed her.

SALOME

It is not my mother's voice that I heed. It is for mine own pleasure that I ask the head of Iokanaan in a silver charger. You have sworn an oath, Herod. Forget not that you have sworn an oath.

HEROD

I know it. I have sworn an oath by my gods. I know it well. But I pray thee, Salome, ask of me something else. Ask of me the half of my kingdom, and I will give it thee. But ask not of me what thy lips have asked.

SALOME

I ask of you the head of Iokanaan.

HEROD

No, no, I will not give it thee.

SALOME

You have sworn an oath, Herod.

HERODIAS

Yes, you have sworn an oath. Everybody heard you. You swore it before everybody.

HEROD

Peace, woman! It is not to you I speak.

HERODIAS

My daughter has done well to ask the head of Iokanaan. He has covered me with insults. He has said unspeakable things against me. One can see that she loves her mother well. Do not yield, my daughter. He has sworn on oath, he has sworn an oath.

HEROD

Peace! Speak not to me! ... Salome, I pray thee be not stubborn. I have ever been kind toward thee. I have ever loved thee. ... It may be that I have loved thee too much. Therefore ask not this thing of me. This is a terrible thing, an awful thing to ask of me. Surely, I think thou art jesting. The head of a man that is cut from his body is ill to look upon, is it not? It is not meet that the eyes of a virgin should look upon such a thing. What pleasure couldst thou have in it? There is no pleasure that thou couldst have in it. No, no, it is not that thou desirest. Hearken to me. I have an emerald, a great emerald and round, that the minion of Cæsar has sent unto me. When thou lookest through this emerald thou canst see that which passeth afar off. Cæsar himself carries such an emerald when he goes to the circus. But my emerald is the larger. I know well that it is the larger. It is the largest emerald in the whole world. Thou wilt take that, wilt thou not? Ask it of me and I will give it thee.

SALOME

I demand the head of Iokanaan.

HEROD

Thou art not listening. Thou art not listening. Suffer me to speak, Salome.

[45]

that I ask the head of Jokanaan in a silver charger. You have sworn an oath, Herod. Forget not that you have sworn an oath.

HEROD

I know it. I have sworn an oath by my gods. I know it well. But I pray thee, Salome, ask of me something else. Ask of me the half of my kingdom, and I will give it thee. But ask not of me what thy lips have asked.

SALOME

I ask of you the head of Jokanaan.

HEROD

No, no, I will not give it thee.

SALOME

You have sworn an oath, Herod.

HERODIAS

Yes, you have sworn an oath. Everybody heard you. You swore it before everybody.

HEROD

Peace, woman! It is not to you I speak.

HERODIAS

My daughter has done well to ask the head of Jokanaan. He has covered me with insults. He has said unspeakable things against me. One can see that she loves her mother well. Do not yield, my daughter. He has sworn on oath, he has sworn an oath.

HEROD

Peace! Speak not to me! . . . Salome, I pray thee be not stubborn. I have ever been kind toward thee. I have ever loved thee. . . . It may be that I have loved thee too much. Therefore ask not this thing of me. This is a terrible thing, an awful thing to ask of me. Surely, I think thou art jesting. The head of a man that is cut from his body is ill to look upon. Is it not? It is not meet that the eyes of a virgin should look upon such a thing. What pleasure couldst thou have in it? There is no pleasure that thou couldst have in it. No, no, it is not that thou desirest. Hearken to me. I have an emerald, a great emerald and round, that the minion of Caesar has sent unto me. When thou lookest through this emerald thou canst see that which passeth afar off. Caesar himself carries such an emerald when he goes to the circus. But my emerald is the larger. I know well that it is the larger. It is the largest emerald in the whole world. Thou wilt take that, wilt thou not? Ask it of me and I will give it thee.

SALOME

I demand the head of Jokanaan.

HEROD

Thou art not listening. Thou art not listening. Suffer me to speak, Salome.

The head of Jokanaan!

HEROD

No, no, thou wouldst not have that. Thou sayest that but to trouble me, because that I have looked at thee and ceased not this night. It is true, I have looked at thee and ceased not this night. Thy beauty has troubled me. Thy beauty has grievously troubled me, and I have looked at thee overmuch. Nay, but I will look at thee no more. One should not look at anything. Neither at things, nor at people should one look. Only in mirrors is it well to look, for mirrors do but show us masks. Oh! oh! bring wine! I thirst ... Salome, Salome, let us be as friends. Bethink thee ... Ah! what would I say? What was't? Ah! I remember it! ... Salome,—nay but come nearer to me; I fear thou wilt not hear my words,—Salome, thou knowest my white peacocks, my beautiful white peacocks, that walk in the garden between the myrtles and the tall cypress-trees. Their beaks are gilded with gold and the grains that they eat are smeared with gold, and their feet are stained with purple. When they cry out the rain comes, and the moon shows herself in the heavens when they spread their tails. Two by two they walk between the cypress-trees and the black myrtles, and each has a slave to tend it. Sometimes they fly across the trees, and anon they couch in the grass, and round the pools of the water. There are not in all the world birds so wonderful. I know that Caesar himself has no birds so fair as my birds. I will give thee fifty of my peacocks. They will follow thee whithersoever thou goest, and in the midst of them thou wilt be like unto the moon in the midst of a great white cloud.... I will give them to thee, all. I have but a hundred, and in the whole world there is no king who has peacocks like unto my peacocks. But I will give them all to thee. Only thou must loose me from my oath, and must not ask of me that which thy lips have asked of me.

[He empties the cup of wine.]

SALOME

Give me the head of Jokanaan!

HERODIAS

Well said, my daughter! As for you, you are ridiculous with your peacocks.

HEROD

Peace! you are always crying out. You cry out like a beast of prey. You must not cry in such fashion. Your voice wearies me. Peace, I tell you! ... Salome, think on what thou art doing. It may be that this man comes from God. He is a holy man. The finger of God has touched him. God has put terrible words into his mouth. In the palace, as in the desert, God is ever with him.... It may

SALOME

The head of Iokanaan!

HEROD

No, no, thou wouldst not have that. Thou sayest that but to
trouble me, because that I have looked at thee and ceased not this
night. It is true, I have looked at thee and ceased not this night.
Thy beauty has troubled me. Thy beauty has grievously troubled
me, and I have looked at thee overmuch. Nay, but I will look at
thee no more. One should not look at anything. Neither at things,
nor at people should one look. Only in mirrors is it well to look,
for mirrors do but show us masks. Oh! oh! bring wine! I thirst.
. . . Salome, Salome, let us be as friends. Bethink thee. . . . Ah!
what would I say? What was't? Ah! I remember it! . . . Salome,
—nay but come nearer to me; I fear thou wilt not hear my words,
—Salome, thou knowest my white peacocks, my beautiful white
peacocks, that walk in the garden between the myrtles and the
tall cypress-trees. Their beaks are gilded with gold and the grains
that they eat are smeared with gold, and their feet are stained
with purple. When they cry out the rain comes, and the moon
shows herself in the heavens when they spread their tails. Two
by two they walk between the cypress-trees and the black myrtles,
and each has a slave to tend it. Sometimes they fly across the trees,
and anon they couch in the grass, and round the pools of the
water. There are not in all the world birds so wonderful. I know
that Cæsar himself has no birds so fair as my birds. I will give
thee fifty of my peacocks. They will follow thee whithersoever
thou goest, and in the midst of them thou wilt be like unto the
moon in the midst of a great white cloud. . . . I will give them
to thee, all. I have but a hundred, and in the whole world there
is no king who has peacocks like unto my peacocks. But I will
give them all to thee. Only thou must loose me from my oath, and
must not ask of me that which thy lips have asked of me.

[*He empties the cup of wine.*]

SALOME

Give me the head of Iokanaan!

HERODIAS

Well said, my daughter! As for you, you are ridiculous with your
peacocks.

HEROD

Peace! you are always crying out. You cry out like a beast of prey.
You must not cry in such fashion. Your voice wearies me. Peace,
I tell you! . . . Salome, think on what thou art doing. It may be
that this man comes from God. He is a holy man. The finger of
God has touched him. God has put terrible words into his mouth.
In the palace, as in the desert, God is ever with him. . . . It may

[46]

be that He is, at least. One cannot tell, but is possible that God is with him and for him. If he die also, peradventure some evil may befall me. Verily, he has said that evil will befall some one on the day whereon he dies. On whom should it fall if it fall not on me? Remember, I slipped in blood when I came hither. Also did I not hear a beating of wings in the air, a beating of vast wings? These are ill omens. And there were other things. I am sure that there were other things, though I saw them not. Thou wouldst not that some evil should befall me, Salome? Listen to me again.

SALOME

Give me the head of Iokanaan!

HEROD

Ah! thou art not listening to me. Be calm. As for me, am I not calm? I am altogether calm. Listen. I have jewels hidden in this place—jewels that thy mother even has never seen; jewels that are marvellous to look at. I have a collar of pearls, set in four rows. They are like unto moons chained with rays of silver. They are even as half a hundred moons caught in a golden net. On the ivory breast of a queen they have rested. Thou shalt be as fair as a queen when thou wearest them. I have amethysts of two kinds; one that is black like wine, and one that is red like wine that one has coloured with water. I have topazes yellow as are the eyes of tigers, and topazes that are pink as the eyes of a wood-pigeon, and green topazes that are as the eyes of cats. I have opals that burn always, with a flame that is cold as ice, opals that make sad men's minds, and are afraid of the shadows. I have onyxes like the eyeballs of a dead woman. I have moonstones that change when the moon changes, and are wan when they see the sun. I have sapphires big like eggs, and as blue as blue flowers. The sea wanders within them, and the moon comes never to trouble the blue of their waves. I have chrysolites and beryls, and chryso-prases and rubies; I have sardonyx and hyacinth stones, and stones of chalcedony, and I will give them all unto thee, all, and other things will I add to them. The King of the Indies has but even now sent me four fans fashioned from the feathers of par-rots, and the King of Numidia a garment of ostrich feathers. I have a crystal, into which it is not lawful for a woman to look, nor may young men behold it until they have been beaten with rods. In a coffer of nacre I have three wondrous turquoises. He who wears them on his forehead can imagine things which are not, and he who carries them in his hand can turn the fruitful woman into a woman that is barren. These are great treasures. They are treasures above all price. But this is not all. In an ebony coffer I have two cups of amber that are like apples of pure gold.

If an enemy pour poison into these cups they become like apples of silver. In a coffer incrusted with amber I have sandals incrusted with glass. I have mantles that have been brought from the land of the Seres, and bracelets decked about with carbuncles and with jade that come from the city of Euphrates. . . . What desirest thou more than this, Salome? Tell me the thing that thou desirest, and I will give it thee. All that thou askest I will give thee, save one thing only. I will give thee all that is mine, save only the life of one man. I will give thee the mantle of the high priest. I will give thee the veil of the sanctuary.

THE JEW

Oh! oh!

SALOME

Give me the head of Iokanaan!

HEROD

[*Sinking back in his seat.*] Let her be given what she asks! Of a truth she is her mother's child! [*The first Soldier approaches. Herodias draws from the hand of the Tetrarch the ring of death, and gives it to the Soldier, who straightway bears it to the Executioner. The Executioner looks scared.*] Who has taken my ring? There was a ring on my right hand. Who has drunk my wine? There was wine in my cup. It was full of wine. Some one has drunk it! Oh! surely some evil will befall some one. [*The Executioner goes down into the cistern.*] Ah! wherefore did I give my oath? Hereafter let no king swear an oath. If he keep it not, it is terrible, and if he keep it, it is terrible also.

HERODIAS

My daughter has done well.

HEROD

I am sure that some misfortune will happen.

SALOME

[*She leans over the cistern and listens.*] There is no sound. I hear nothing. Why does he not cry out, this man? Ah! if any man sought to kill me, I would cry out, I would struggle, I would not suffer. . . . Strike, strike, Naaman, strike, I tell you. . . . No, I hear nothing. There is a silence, a terrible silence. Ah! something has fallen upon the ground. I heard something fall. It was the sword of the executioner. He is afraid, this slave. He has dropped his sword. He dares not kill him. He is a coward, this slave! Let soldiers be sent. [*She sees the Page of Herodias and addresses him.*] Come hither. Thou wert the friend of him who is dead, wert thou not? Well, I tell thee, there are not dead men enough. Go to the soldiers and bid them go down and bring me the thing I ask, the thing the Tetrarch has promised me, the thing that is mine. [*The Page recoils. She turns to the soldiers.*] Hither, ye soldiers. Get ye down into this cistern and bring me the head of this man. Tetrarch, Tetrarch,

command your soldiers that they bring me the head of Iokanaan.

[A huge black arm, the arm of the Executioner, comes forth from the cistern, bearing on a silver shield the head of Iokanaan. Salome seizes it. Herod hides his face with his cloak. Herodias smiles and fans herself. The Nazarenes fall on their knees and begin to pray.]

Ah! thou wouldst not suffer me to kiss thy mouth, Iokanaan. Well! I will kiss it now, I will bite it with my teeth as one bites a ripe fruit. Yes, I will kiss thy mouth, Iokanaan. I said it; did I not say it? I said it. Ah! I will kiss it now.... But wherefore dost thou not look at me, Iokanaan? Thine eyes that were so terrible, so full of rage and scorn, are shut now. Wherefore are they shut? Open thine eyes! Lift up thine eyelids, Iokanaan! Wherefore dost thou not look at me? Art thou afraid of me, Iokanaan, that thou wilt not look at me?... And thy tongue, that was like a red snake darting poison, it moves no more, it speaks no words, Iokanaan, that scarlet viper that spat its venom upon me. It is strange, is it not? How is it that the red viper stirs no longer? ...Thou wouldst have none of me, Iokanaan. Thou rejectedst me. Thou didst speak evil words against me. Thou didst bear thyself toward me as to a harlot, as to a woman that is a wanton, to me, Salome, daughter of Herodias, Princess of Judæa! Well, I still live, but thou art dead, and thy head belongs to me. I can do with it what I will. I can throw it to the dogs and to the birds of the air. That which the dogs leave, the birds of the air shall devour.... Ah, Iokanaan, Iokanaan, thou wert the man that I loved alone among men! All other men were hateful to me. But thou wert beautiful. Thy body was a column of ivory set upon feet of silver. It was a garden full of doves and lilies of silver. It was a tower of silver decked with shields of ivory. There was nothing in the world so white as thy body. There was nothing in the world so black as thy hair. In the whole world there was nothing so red as thy mouth. Thy voice was a censer that scattered strange perfumes, and when I looked on thee I heard a strange music. Ah! wherefore didst thou not look at me, Iokanaan? With the cloak of thine hands, and with the cloak of thy blasphemies thou didst hide thy face. Thou didst put upon thine eyes the covering of him who would see his God. Well, thou hast seen thy God, Iokanaan, but me, me, thou didst never see. If thou hadst seen me thou hadst loved me. I saw thee, and I loved thee. Oh, how I loved thee! I love thee yet, Iokanaan. I love only thee.... I am athirst for thy beauty; I am hungry for thy body; and neither wine nor apples can appease my desire. What shall I do now, Iokanaan? Neither the floods nor the great waters can quench my passion. I was a princess, and thou didst scorn me. I was a virgin, and thou didst take my virginity from me. I was chaste, and thou didst fill my veins with fire. ... Ah! ah! wherefore didst thou not look at me? If thou hadst looked at me thou hadst loved me. Well I know that thou wouldst have loved me, and the mystery of Love is greater than the mystery of Death.

HEROD

She is monstrous, thy daughter; I tell thee she is monstrous. In truth, what she has done is a great crime. I am sure that it is a crime against some unknown God.

HERODIAS

I am well pleased with my daughter. She has done well. And I would stay here now.

HEROD

[*Rising.*] Ah! There speaks my brother's wife! Come! I will not stay in this place. Come, I tell thee. Surely some terrible thing will befall. Manasseh, Issachar, Ozias, put out the torches. I will not look at things, I will not suffer things to look at me. Put out the torches! Hide the moon! Hide the stars! Let us hide ourselves in our palace, Herodias. I begin to be afraid.

[*The slaves put out the torches. The stars disappear. A great cloud crosses the moon and conceals it completely. The stage becomes quite dark. The Tetrarch begins to climb the staircase.*]

THE VOICE OF SALOME

Ah! I have kissed thy mouth, Iokanaan, I have kissed thy mouth. There was a bitter taste on thy lips. Was it the taste of blood? ... Nay; but perchance it was the taste of love. ... They say that love hath a bitter taste. ... But what matter? what matter? I have kissed thy mouth, Iokanaan, I have kissed thy mouth.

[*A ray of moonlight falls on Salome and illumines her.*]

HEROD

[*Turning round and seeing Salome.*] Kill that woman!

[*The soldiers rush forward and crush beneath their shields Salome, daughter of Herodias, Princess of Judæa.*]

[51]

didst fill my veins with fire. ... Ah! ah! wherefore didst thou not look at me? If thou hadst looked at me thou hadst loved me. Well I know that thou wouldst have loved me, and the mystery of Love is greater than the mystery of Death.

HEROD

She is monstrous, thy daughter; I tell thee she is monstrous. In truth, what she has done is a great crime. I am sure that it is a crime against some unknown God.

HERODIAS

I am well pleased with my daughter. She has done well. And I would stay here now.

HEROD

[Rising.] Ah! There speaks my brother's wife! Come! I will not stay in this place. Come, I tell thee. Surely some terrible thing will befall. Manasseh, Issachar, Ozias, put out the torches. I will not look at things, I will not suffer things to look at me. Put out the torches! Hide the moon! Hide the stars! Let us hide ourselves in our palace, Herodias. I begin to be afraid.

[The slaves put out the torches. The stars disappear. A great cloud crosses the moon and conceals it completely. The stage becomes quite dark. The Tetrarch begins to climb the staircase.]

THE VOICE OF SALOME

Ah! I have kissed thy mouth, Iokanaan, I have kissed thy mouth. There was a bitter taste on thy lips. Was it the taste of blood? ... Nay; but perchance it was the taste of love. ... They say that love hath a bitter taste. ... But what matter? what matter? I have kissed thy mouth, Iokanaan, I have kissed thy mouth.

[A ray of moonlight falls on Salome and illumines her.]

HEROD

[Turning round and seeing Salome.] Kill that woman!

[The soldiers rush forward and crush beneath their shields Salome, daughter of Herodias, Princess of Judaea.]